Word Analysis

The
**READING
PUZZLE**

Elaine K. McEwan
Linda M. Nielsen
Robert Edison

CORWIN PRESS
Classroom

For information:

Corwin Press
A SAGE Company
2455 Teller Road
Thousand Oaks, California 91320
CorwinPress.com

SAGE, Ltd.
1 Oliver's Yard
55 City Road
London EC1Y 1SP
United Kingdom

SAGE India Pvt. Ltd.
B 1/I 1 Mohan Cooperative
Industrial Area
Mathura Road, New Delhi
India 110 044

SAGE Asia-Pacific Pvt. Ltd.
33 Pekin Street #02-01
Far East Square
Singapore 048763

ISBN: 978-1-4129-5825-7

This book is printed on acid-free paper.

08 09 10 11 12 10 9 8 7 6 5 4 3 2 1

Executive Editor: Kathleen Hex
Managing Developmental Editor: Christine Hood
Editorial Assistant: Anne O'Dell
Developmental Writers: Linda M. Nielsen and Robert Edison
Developmental Editor: Collene Dobelmann
Proofreader: Carrie Reiling
Art Director: Anthony D. Paular
Design Project Manager: Jeffrey Stith
Cover Designers: Michael Dubowe and Jeffrey Stith
Illustrator: Mark Mason
Design Consultant: The Development Source

Acknowledgements
from Elaine McEwan:
To the teachers who teach all of their students to read.

Acknowledgements
from Linda Nielsen:
A special thanks to Daneva Dansby of K. R. Martindale Show Management for her creative stories. Much appreciation also to my very supportive husband, Jim Nielsen, whose background and knowledge as an educator provided the perfect sounding board.

TABLE OF CONTENTS

Introduction

Welcome to the world of word analysis! This resource focuses on two areas of learning: essential linguistic patterns (variations in how letters are pronounced) and essential morphographs (variations of what letters or groups of letters mean, such as prefixes, suffixes, and roots).

The goal of the Linguistics section of this book is to assist students in becoming fluent decoders. Students will learn patterns that they can use to aid them in their decoding speed. Some targeted linguistic patterns are spelling patterns that students often see in print but have more than one common pronunciation. To become proficient readers, students must first become aware of the different pronunciations and then practice them with speed and fluency. Practice only makes perfect if students are practicing the perfect pronunciations.

The Linguistics section includes activities with an oral component. When students can look at a word and pronounce it without thinking about how to decode it, they can focus all their energy on comprehension. The goal of these linguistics activities is for students to internalize the pronunciations of spelling patterns and decode words automatically. The activities are geared for whole-class participation and are designed to accommodate 35 students per class.

Linguistics also includes the study of heteronyms. Heteronyms are words that are spelled the same but have different meanings and pronunciations. Studying heteronyms will be an entertaining challenge.

The goal of the Morphology section of this book is to hone students' word analysis skills. Morphology is the branch of linguistics that focuses on word structure and the changes in forms of words. A morphograph, or morpheme, is the smallest linguistic unit of meaning for a word. Morphographs include:

- Real words, or root words, such as *man* and *can*

- Non-word Latin and Greek roots, such as *aqua,* meaning *water* (Latin), and *auto,* meaning *self* (Greek)

- Prefixes such as *pre-,* meaning *before*

- Suffixes such as *-less,* meaning *without*

This resource includes lists of common Latin and Greek roots as well as prefixes and suffixes. Students will participate in both written and interactive activities to help them decipher unfamiliar words once they have memorized the meanings of roots, prefixes, and suffixes. Students will discover what a powerful tool knowledge can be.

Put It Into Practice

Pronunciations of English words are predictable; 84% of these words have a regular spelling pattern (Blevins, 1998). Therefore, students must become familiar with the spelling patterns that represent different sounds in the English language—the study of linguistics. Students will discover that one spelling pattern may represent different sounds and that one sound may have different spelling patterns.

Linguistic difficulties become more evident in the upper grades. Often, teachers assume that students will internalize spelling patterns through increased independent reading, so they do not formally teach phonemic awareness of more difficult words. This can present problems for students who are not fluent in English, who do not like to read, or who do not speak English as a first language. In order for students to comprehend the material they read, they must read with fluency. Fluent readers must decode linguistic patterns automatically with a rapid pace so that all of their effort focuses on understanding what the words mean, not on pronouncing them.

Strategies used to increase decoding and fluency skills are an important piece of the Reading Puzzle, a way of organizing and understanding reading instruction, as introduced in my book, *Teach Them All to Read: Catching the Kids Who Fall Through the Cracks* (2002). The puzzle contains the essential reading skills that students need to master in order to become literate at every grade level. *The Reading Puzzle, Grades 4–8* series focuses on five of these skills: Spelling, Fluency, Comprehension, Vocabulary, and Word Analysis.

I also underscore two key factors for solving the Reading Puzzle: the importance of fluency and reading materials with linguistic patterns that students have been taught to decode.

"[They] are inextricably linked to one another . . . Students will not gain the fluency they need to become literate without reading a lot, but students whose oral reading is slow and inaccurate because of inaccurate word identification skills or speed deficiencies are unlikely to read enough voluntarily to become fluent readers. Many students fall through the cracks at precisely this point on the literacy continuum. Even those students who know how to phonemically decode can fall through the cracks if the books they choose or are given to read do not support their current reading levels" (McEwan, 2002, p. 49).

> **Teaching reading effectively requires mastery of linguistic patterns with fluency and speed.**

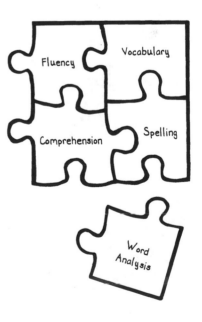

In other words, teaching reading effectively requires mastery of linguistic patterns with fluency and speed. Moreover, the greater the volume of material read, the more the linguistic patterns become internalized and the less time students have to spend on decoding. Thus, students' time and energy can now be focused on comprehension.

In the 2006 film, *Akeelah and the Bee*, the professor who serves as Akeelah's spelling coach and mentor impresses upon her the importance of knowing Latin and Greek roots, as well as prefixes and suffixes, in learning how to spell. Learning roots, prefixes, and suffixes enables students to think of how unknown words are put together. National standards similarly emphasize the importance of knowing these roots and affixes as a means of developing vocabulary, thus enhancing comprehension.

> **Understanding roots and affixes aids students in non-classroom vocabulary development.**

With a working knowledge of common roots and affixes, students can increase their ability to understand and comprehend words they have not previously seen in that exact format. Students can only maintain grade-level progress by learning 3,000 to 5,000 new words per year, far more than can ever be taught in a classroom situation. Furthermore, if students are to acquire the word meanings they need to read with understanding, they must not only read a lot, they must also learn how to become independent word learners (McEwan, 2002, p. 71). Word analysis through the understanding of roots and affixes is one powerful tool that aids students in non-classroom vocabulary development.

In addition, knowledge of word analysis enables students to take one form of a word and use it appropriately as a different part of speech, thereby giving them greater flexibility in their writing techniques. There are many more roots and affixes than are covered in this book, but those that are included represent roots and affixes students encounter most frequently. The prefixes and suffixes in particular are found in a large percentage of words that most students will encounter throughout their school experience. Learning these roots and affixes will provide students with a solid foundation for improved word analysis skills in both reading and writing.

The improvement of student reading abilities is of the utmost importance among both state and national educational goals. By focusing on both the skills necessary to go beyond mere word decoding through linguistic practice and development, as well as the specific areas of word analysis through roots and affixes that can enhance reading comprehension, this resource will help to facilitate maximum success. As a result, students will become more enthusiastic lifelong readers and learners.

Pronunciation Patterns

Pair Me Up

The more decoding tools students possess, the better their potential for reading comprehension. Use the following activity to raise students' awareness of the relationship between certain pairs of letters. Students will say five pairs of consonants using the same mouth, tongue, and teeth positions. The only difference between the two sounds is that one sound is quiet and the other is noisy.

Write the consonant pairs below on the board. Point to the first letter (*f*) and have students say that sound. Tell students that this is a "quiet" sound. Direct them to keep their mouth positions the same and see if they can make the sound of the other letter (*v*). Point out that this is a "noisier" sound than the first.

Consonant Pairs

Quiet Sounds	Noisy Sounds
f	v
k	g
t	d
p	b
s	z

Ask students to place their fingers lightly on the front of their throat and repeat the letter sounds. As they say the noisy consonant, they will feel a vibration. Continue with the other consonant pairs.

Say words that begin with each consonant pair so students can familiarize themselves with the similar sounds. Have students list five words that begin with each consonant.

Write all consonant pairs on separate index cards (e.g., *f* on one card, *v* on one card, and so on) and shuffle the cards. Choose a student to draw a card and show it to a classmate. That student must say a word that begins with the "companion" letter shown on the card. For example, if the letter is *f*, the student must say a word that begins with *v*. If a correct response is not given within a certain amount of time, the student sits down. Decide how much response time is appropriate (e.g., five seconds) and set a timer. Continue the game by inviting a new student to draw a card. Follow-up this activity by having students complete the **I Know My Consonant Pairs reproducible (page 8)**.

I Know My Consonant Pairs

Directions: Write the letter that completes each consonant pair.

1. b _____

2. t _____

3. v _____

4. s _____

5. g _____

Directions: Write *quiet* or *noisy* to describe each consonant.

6. b _____   7. v _____

8. g _____   9. k _____

10. z _____   11. d _____

12. t _____   13. s _____

14. f _____   15. p _____

Directions: Match the words that begin with letters that are consonant pairs. Write the letter of the matching word on the line.

16. determined _____   **A.** funny

17. kangaroo _____   **B.** game

18. victorious _____   **C.** telescope

19. zoo _____   **D.** balloon

20. portable _____   **E.** submarine

Word Sorts

"Word Sorts" are a great way to test students' knowledge of word pronunciations and to increase their speed of reading the words. Use "Word Sorts" to practice the linguistic patterns *ch, ea, ed,* and *s.* The basic structure of the activity remains the same; just substitute the word cards for the pattern on which you'd like to focus. Alter teaching cues as necessary. Repeat each "Word Sort" several times and challenge students to increase their speed.

Linguistic Patterns

ch = /ch/ /sh/ /k/
ea = /ĕ/ /ē/
ed = /t/ /d/ /əd/
s = /s/ /z/

Prior to the activity, copy onto cardstock a class set of the reproducibles **ch Word Cards (page 10)**, **ea Word Cards (page 12)**, **ed Word Cards (page 14)**, and **s Word Cards (page 16)**. Give each student four resealable plastic bags and the Word Cards reproducibles. Then instruct students to cut apart each set of words, put them in a bag, and label the bag with the corresponding linguistic pattern.

Write the linguistic pattern *ch* on the board. Then write the different pronunciations the pattern makes. *(/ch/, /sh/, /k/)* Ask students to give examples of words for each pronunciation and list them on the board (e.g., *reach, machine, ache*). When students are familiar with the linguistic pattern and its pronunciations, begin the "Word Sort."

Tell students that when you say *sort,* they will organize the words from the *ch* bag in like-pronunciation columns exactly as the headings are listed on the board. Have volunteers read the words aloud to make sure they are in the correct columns. Then continue with the linguistic patterns *ea, ed,* and *s.*

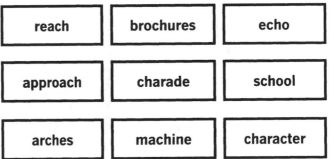

Prior to the activity, make transparencies of the reproducibles **Three Pronunciations of ch (page 11)**, **Two Pronunciations of ea (page 13)**, **Three Pronunciations of ed (page 15)**, and **Two Pronunciations of s (page 17)**. Display each transparency on the overhead, one at a time, but keep it covered until students finish sorting. When students have finished, ask them to compare their work to the list on the overhead. Have students rearrange their words so the order matches that on the transparency. Say the words in each column together quickly. Then call on students to say the words again quickly and accurately.

As a follow-up to "Word Sorts," give students a copy of the **A Recipe for Friendship reproducible (page 18)**. Invite them to read the story and then use the **Word Sort Review reproducible (page 19)** to sort the boldface words by linguistic pattern and pronunciation.

ch Word Cards

character	approach	chemistry
cache	achieve	which
chocolate	chandelier	brochure
Cheyenne	chauffeur	bellyache
schedule	speech	fuchsia
chorus	scholarship	school
reach	echo	arches
machine	charade	chlorine

Reproducible

Three Pronunciations of *ch*

/ch/	/sh/	/k/
reach	brochure	bellyache
chocolate	chandelier	schedule
achieve	machine	school
approach	chauffeur	scholarship
which	Cheyenne	chorus
arches	charade	character
speech	cache	echo
	fuchsia	chemistry
		chlorine

ea Word Cards

breath		leave
cream	ready	bread
beneath	sea	weather
sweat	dream	heavy
feather	breakfast	treasure
eagle	head	conceal

Reproducible

Two Pronunciations of ea

/ē/	/ĕ/
leave	head
easy	sweat
cream	bread
conceal	weather
eagle	heavy
sea	treasure
beneath	ready
dream	breakfast
	feather
	breath

ed Word Cards

wondered	picked	interested
jumped	handed	wanted
hoped	stared	clapped
tried	received	discovered
blinked	cheered	showed
started	worried	finished
graduated	patted	nodded
curved	worked	dropped

Reproducible   978-1-4129-5825-7 • © Corwin Press

Three Pronunciations of *ed*

/t/	/d/	/əd/
dropped	stared	wanted
picked	worried	handed
blinked	curved	started
finished	showed	nodded
hoped	cheered	patted
jumped	discovered	interested
clapped	received	graduated
worked	tried	
	wondered	

s Word Cards

let's	less	is	bikes
things	thanks	yes	roses
across	please	grass	that's
friends	class	arms	boys
was	as	checks	motorcycles
cheese	lakes	windows	pockets

Reproducible   978-1-4129-5825-7 • © *Corwin Press*

Two Pronunciations of *s*

/s/	/z/
bikes	boys
pockets	arms
less	roses
let's	friends
class	as
yes	motorcycles
across	things
thanks	please
checks	was
that's	is
grass	windows
lakes	cheese

A Recipe for Friendship

Directions: Read the story. Write the boldface words in the correct columns of the Word Sort Review chart.

The two **girls** had been **friends** since the first day of school. The **teacher assigned** them **desks across** from **each** other at the back of the **class**. **Charlotte** was the quieter of the pair, with an **easy smile** and a **head** for **scholarship**, especially math. She had the sort of **character** that **approached** any **challenge as** if it **was** little more than a **simple** equation of **numbers** to be **added** up and **checked**.

Heather had little patience for arithmetic, although she **discovered** some **charm** in **chemistry**. It **reminded** her of the creative mixing of cooking: blend a **measure** of sugar, a cup of **cream**, flour, a **pinch** of **salt**, a shave of **chocolate**, and a few **cherries**, and the **nose** would be **greeted** with that wonderful **heavy** smell like that of **bread** baking before **breakfast**. She wouldn't dare **eat** some of the **mixtures** they **brewed** in chemistry class—bubbling, oozing **things** that would surely give you a **bellyache**—but the **experiments** were **recipes** all the same, and she **wanted** to be a **chef** one day.

The **room's** only window **arched** at the back of the class. Charlotte often **looked** out through the **clear glass**, gazing into the **sea** of sky that **showed** itself blue or **sometimes** gray, depending on the **weather**. **Beneath** the window was the **grassy** escape of the **school's fields**, **lined** with **leafy trees** and **caches** of empty **bikes** patiently awaiting the return of their **owners**. It wasn't that Charlotte **was** lazy, or even **uninterested**, but sometimes she found herself **daydreaming**.

The teacher had a distinct pattern of **speech**, and **combined** with the **clipped exclamations** of **chalk** hitting the board, his voice usually **roused** her from her **daydream** (but not **always**).

This **exchange** was how the girls' friendship **cemented** itself on that first day of **school**:

"**Miss**, **please** tell us the compound for the element *chlorine*," the teacher said.

Charlotte **started** to **answer** and then **stopped**; all **heads** were **turned** in her direction. Her **cheeks burned** a **rosy** red.

"Cl," Heather **piped** up.

"Good, although next time **let's hear** your **friend's thoughts**," the teacher replied.

"**Thanks**," Charlotte **mouthed**. A friendship was **created**—one that would **always** bake just right **because it's** the mixing **that's** the art, not the actual **numbers**.

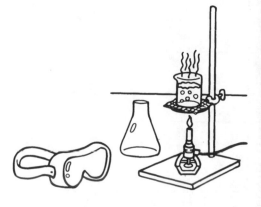

Word Sort Review

Directions: Read "A Recipe for Friendship." Write each boldface word in the column with the correct pronunciation.

Hint: Some of the words belong in more than one column.

/z/	/s/	/əd/	/d/	/t/	/ē/	/ĕ/	/k/	/sh/	/ch/

Positive Pronunciation Board Game

Encourage good classroom behavior while reinforcing the pronunciations of words from previous "Word Sort" activities or any word lists you generate with students in class.

Copy the **Positive Pronunciation Game Board reproducibles (pages 21–22)**. Tape the pages together to create the game board and laminate it for durability. Make several game boards if you want more than one group to play at a time. Provide four game markers and one die for each game board. Write vocabulary words you wish to review on index cards. Tell students that four players can participate at each game board.

Explain to students the instructions for the game.

1. Players place the cards in a facedown stack near the game board and position their game markers on the space labeled *Arrived at school early!*

2. To begin, a player draws a vocabulary card. If the player pronounces the word correctly, he or she rolls the die and moves a game marker that number of spaces on the game board.

3. If the player pronounces the word incorrectly, the next player gets a turn.

4. In order to win, players must roll the exact number needed to land on the last space.

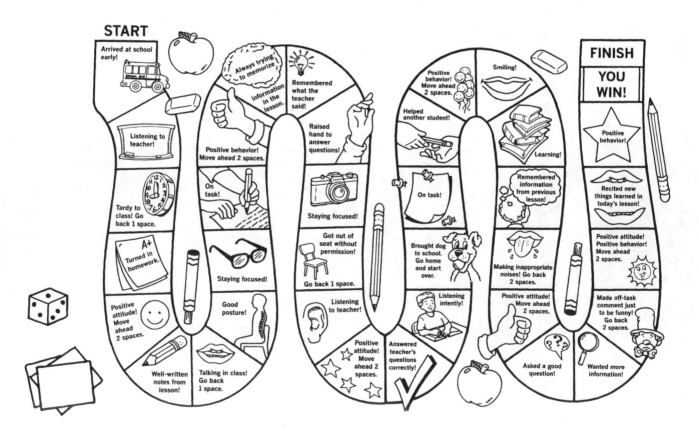

Positive Pronunciation

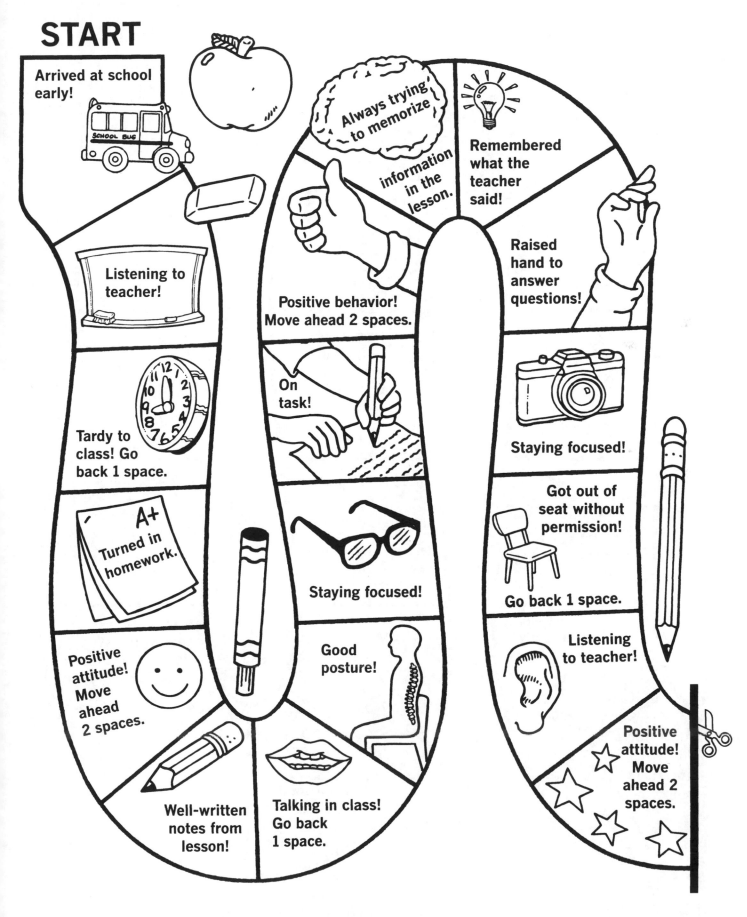

START

Arrived at school early!

Listening to teacher!

Tardy to class! Go back 1 space.

A+ Turned in homework.

Positive attitude! Move ahead 2 spaces.

Well-written notes from lesson!

Always trying to memorize information in the lesson.

Positive behavior! Move ahead 2 spaces.

On task!

Staying focused!

Good posture!

Talking in class! Go back 1 space.

Remembered what the teacher said!

Raised hand to answer questions!

Staying focused!

Got out of seat without permission! Go back 1 space.

Listening to teacher!

Positive attitude! Move ahead 2 spaces.

Game Board

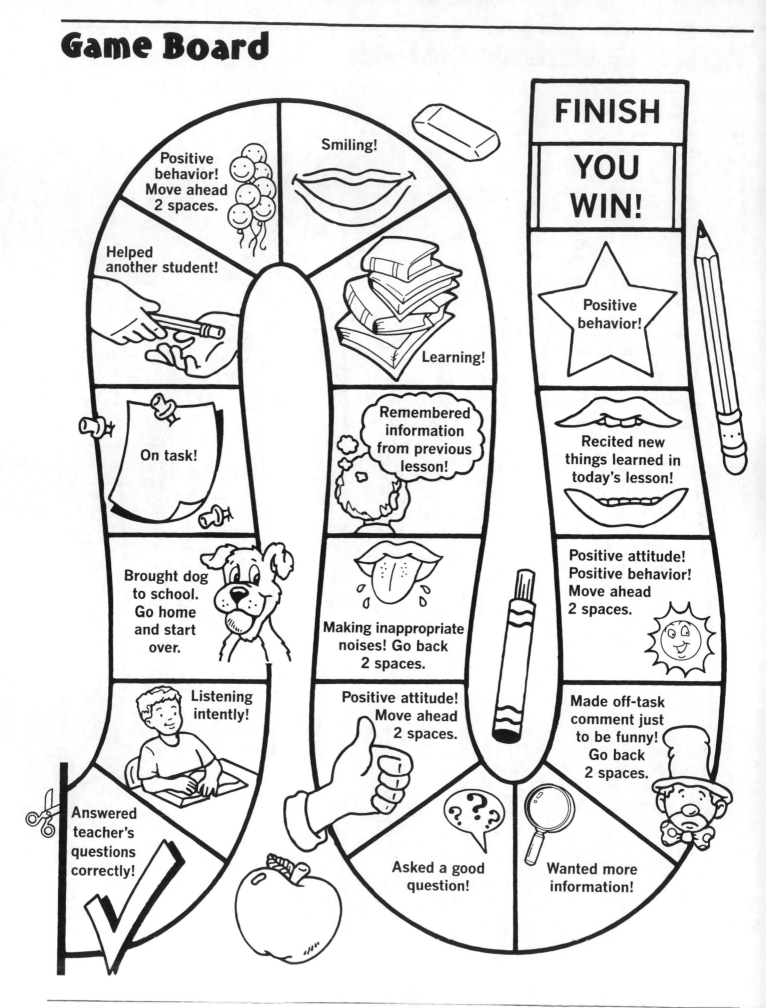

FINISH
YOU WIN!

Positive behavior!

Smiling!

Positive behavior! Move ahead 2 spaces.

Helped another student!

Learning!

Recited new things learned in today's lesson!

On task!

Remembered information from previous lesson!

Positive attitude! Positive behavior! Move ahead 2 spaces.

Brought dog to school. Go home and start over.

Making inappropriate noises! Go back 2 spaces.

Made off-task comment just to be funny! Go back 2 spaces.

Listening intently!

Positive attitude! Move ahead 2 spaces.

Answered teacher's questions correctly!

Asked a good question!

Wanted more information!

oa and ai Spelling Patterns

Young children are often taught: *When two vowels go walking, the first one does the talking, and it says its name*. Although this is not true for all vowel combinations, this is almost always true for the *oa* and *ai* spelling patterns. The following "What Am I?" activity requires students to read these predictable patterns fluently in context.

When the letters *oa* are together in a word, they usually make the long *o* sound. When the letters *ai* are together in a word, they usually make the long *a* sound. The more students practice reading aloud sentences containing target words, the more fluent they will become.

What Am I?

Make a copy of the **"What Am I?" Details reproducibles (pages 24–25)**. Cut apart the cards and distribute them to students. Have students check that they understand all the words and are able to enunciate the sentences clearly. Point out that each sentence contains a boldface word or words with *oa* and/or *ai* spelling patterns.

Have students walk around the room and shake hands with a classmate while reading aloud their sentences. Make sure each student speaks to everyone in the class. Encourage students to listen for context clues to discern the topic of all the sentences.

After everyone has shared their sentences, have students return to their seats. Ask them to guess what all the sentences described and then collect the cards.

Have students recall and write as many details about the African elephant as they can remember. If you wish, give the student with the most details a small prize.

Distribute the cards again and have students read the sentences at their seats. Write the letters *oa* and *ai* on the board as column headings. Ask students to read their sentences aloud to the class and then say the boldface words that contain *oa* or *ai*. Write those words under the appropriate headings. Underline the *oa* or *ai* in each word, say the sound, and then say the word. Repeat the process and invite students to say the sounds and words with you.

Challenge students to tell you the pronunciation rules for the spelling patterns *oa* and *ai*. Congratulate them on their self-discovery!

"What Am I?" Details

People **claim** it is the largest land mammal.	Its **tail** is four feet long with **hair** on the end.	Its body is wrinkled, gray-brown, and has a thin **coat** of **hair**.
It would sink a small **boat** because it can weigh up to 14,000 pounds.	Some **praise** it as the most intelligent mammal.	It likes to **roam** along rivers with its young.
Its hind feet have five toes but only three **nails**.	It loves to spray and **soak** itself with water on a hot day.	It is very smart and uses its **brain** all the time.
Scientists will **explain** that it **boasts** an excellent memory.	Its babies must **wait** 21 or 22 months to be born.	A newborn doesn't need a **coach**. It can follow the herd after just a few days.
A mother can **boast** about having five to six babies in her lifetime.	It needs **soap** because it likes to play in the **rain** and the mud.	It is not **vain**. It uses mud to **coat** and protect its skin from the sun.
It eats almost 300–600 pounds of food **daily**.	It might **fail** to see something because of poor eyesight.	It could **approach** you without making a sound because of its padded feet.

"What Am I?" Details

During the **rainy** season, its **goal** is to find grasses and herbs.	During the dry season, it makes a **road** to a stream to **obtain** leaves, fruit, and bark.	Another **quaint** fact is that it can live to be 60 years old if it **roams** in the wild.
Girls, don't **gloat**, but the matriarch is the head of the herd.	Boys, don't **faint**, but males leave the herd when they are about 13 and travel alone or in bachelor groups.	It communicates with rumbles, growls, bellows, and **moans**.
It can't **wait** for food. It must **roam** to wherever it can find enough food and water.	While wandering the **plains**, its mighty bellow can be heard for miles.	If it stands up **straight**, it can be eleven feet tall.
From its head to its **tail**, it can be 25 feet long.	It once **boasted** a home throughout Africa. Today its **main** home is on reserves.	Since the late 1980s, an international ban on ivory trade **aided** in stopping its population decline.
The largest known of this species is on display at the Smithsonian. At 13 feet tall and 22,000 pounds, it's quite a **load**!	There are 400,000 to 600,000 alive today, although not all **remain** free.	At birth, a baby would be a **pain** to carry. It weighs about 250 pounds!
It won't **float** in the water, but it is an excellent swimmer.	It is in danger of extinction due to **poaching** and loss of habitat.	Sometimes herds can be seen walking together in a long **train**.

y-Sound Strip Books

When representing a vowel sound, the letter *y* can signal that of long *i* or long *e*. At the end of short words (mostly one syllable, but some two syllables), the letter *y* makes a long *i* sound. The letter *y* also makes a long *i* sound in the first syllable of a multisyllabic word. At the end of long words (two-syllable words or words with more than two syllables), the letter *y* makes a long *e* sound. Remind students that *ay* together has a long *a* sound.

Have students make this quick and easy *y*-sound strip book to help them remember the linguistic patterns. Ask students to call out words that end in *y* and write the words on the board. Below is a list of words they might suggest. Ask individual students to read the words. Point to random words (alternating between the columns) to practice fluent decoding abilities with students.

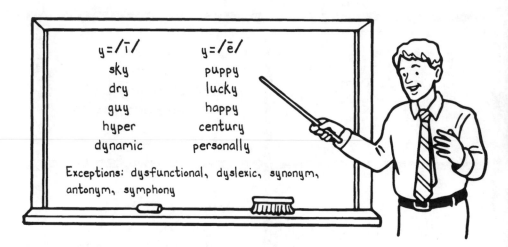

Give each student two sheets of paper and demonstrate how to make a word strip book following these directions:

Hold both papers horizontally. Fold papers in half twice (bringing the long edges together). Cut along the folds so you have eight long strips. Lay all the strips on top of each other. Fold over the strips like a book, leaving the bottom eight pages protruding about three inches from the top eight pages. Staple the pages twice along the fold.

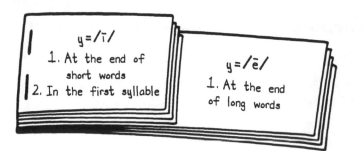

Tell students to title the top short page *y* = /ī/ (1. *At the end of short words* and 2. *In the first syllable*). Have them title the top long page *y* = /ē/ (1. *At the end of long words*). Ask students to write words from the list they generated under the appropriate title (e.g, *dry* belongs on a page beneath *y* = /ī/). If you wish, have students note any exceptions on the back of their *y*-sound strip books.

The Good Goose Is Cool

There is no rule or pattern to teach students when the letters *oo* will make either the sound /o͞o/ or /o͝o/. Words with an *oo* spelling will have an /o͞o/ or an /o͝o/ sound about an equal percentage of the time. Therefore, to promote fluency, students must become familiar with *oo* words and memorize their pronunciations.

Write the Sample Word List of /o͞o/ and /o͝o/ words on the board to practice pronunciation.

Linguistic Patterns

oo has two sounds: /o͞o/ and /o͝o/

Sample Word List

/o͞o/	/o͝o/
balloon	hook
spoon	shook
room	look
moon	book
cool	crook

Divide the class into two teams. Copy the Game Word List onto a transparency. Show only one item (three words) at a time. Team members must quickly and accurately pronounce the words. Give teams one point for each correctly pronounced word for a possible three points per turn. After all the words have been shown, the team with the most points wins. As you play the game, you may wish to circle words that are mispronounced and review them at the end.

Game Word List

1. balloon, brook, moon
2. mood, hoot, foot
3. good, goose, croon
4. too, soot, cook
5. wool, book, drool
6. shoot, goof, hoop
7. nook, coop, doom
8. wood, smooth, noon
9. ooze, rookie, soon
10. woo, shook, snoop
11. moose, moo, look
12. shook, root, kangaroo
13. food, doom, troop
14. shoo, stood, brood
15. groom, football, rookie
16. school, hood, proof
17. toot, droop, zoom
18. brook, woof, tool
19. loot, moot, shook
20. gloom, hook, cookie
21. wool, took, zoo
22. brook, bloom, snooze
23. fool, loose, swoon
24. crook, cook, saloon
25. boom, pool, loon
26. booth, cool, racoon
27. stool, boot, roof
28. loom, loop, tooth
29. broom, hood, stoop
30. loose, igloo, scoop

Now I Know! List

The following activity is designed to familiarize students with the different sounds made by the letter combination *ow*. There is no rule or pattern to teach students when the letters *ow* will make the sound /ou/ or /ō/. Therefore, to promote fluency, students must become familiar with *ow* words and memorize their pronunciations.

Write this sentence on the board: *Now I know!* Underline *ow* in the words. Ask students: *Can you hear a difference in how the **ow** is pronounced?* Discuss their responses. Write on the board /ou/ next to *Now* and /ō/ next to *know*. Ask students to brainstorm other words that have an *ow* spelling with the same pronunciations as *now* and *know*. Have each student write responses on the board under the appropriate column headings.

ow Spelling

Now /ou/	Know /ō/
brow	blow
brown	blown
clown	bowl
cow	bowling
coward	crow
cowboy	flow
dowdy	flown
dower	glow
down	grow
downstairs	grown
downtown	known
frown	low
how	lower
power	show
shower	stow
vow	throw
wow	thrown
flower	tow

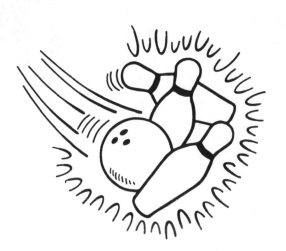

Students may also suggest the words *row*, *bow*, and *sow*. Tell them that these are examples of heteronyms. *Heteronyms* are words that have the same spelling, but their pronunciation changes depending on context and meaning. Stress to students that *row*, *bow*, and *sow* can belong in both lists.

Once students have finished brainstorming, underline *ow* in each word, say the sound *ow* makes in the word, and then say the word. Repeat with each word and have students say the sounds and words with you.

On individual index cards, write words that contain *ow*. Include equal numbers of the pronunciations /ou/ and /ō/. Make one card for each student. Tell students to lay the cards facedown on their desks. Designate half the as room the /ou/ area and the other half of the room as the /ō/ area. Tell students that when you say /ou/ or /ō/, they must silently read the word on their card, decide whether it has the sound /ou/ or /ō/, and go to the corresponding side of the room.

After everyone has arrived at the correct side of the room, have students read aloud the words on their cards. Then have each group of students stand in alphabetical order and read their words again. You may wish to ask for volunteers to read the words belonging to the other group.

Next, tape the index cards on the board. Have students work in pairs to write and illustrate a story or a poem that includes words that contain the *ow* spelling with both pronunciations. Encourage students to read their stories and poems aloud to the class when they are finished. Listen for the correct pronunciations and other decoding and fluency skills.

The cowboy wiped his sweaty brow as the sun sank low in the sky.

Another Way to Spell /ou/

Students should now understand that the spelling pattern *ow* can be pronounced /ou/ and /ō/. Show students that the spelling pattern *ou* also makes the /ou/ sound (e.g., *shout*, *about*, *out*).

Write /ou/ on the board to introduce the linguistic pattern for the lesson. Review words spelled with *ow* that are pronounced with the /ou/ sound. Write on the board *ow = /ou/* as a heading and ask students to list some words from the previous activity to demonstrate that spelling pattern. Underline the *ow* letter combination in each word. Then write the spelling pattern *ou = /ou/* as another heading. Discuss words that have that spelling pattern and are pronounced with the sound /ou/. Write *shout*, *about*, and *out* in that column and underline the *ou* spelling pattern. Ask students to suggest other words with the *ou* spelling pattern that are pronounced with the sound /ou/.

/ou/ Words

ow = /ou/	ou = /ou/
c<u>ow</u>	sh<u>ou</u>t
c<u>ow</u>boy	ab<u>ou</u>t
c<u>ow</u>ard	<u>ou</u>t
h<u>ow</u>	m<u>ou</u>th
w<u>ow</u>	gr<u>ou</u>nd

Practice reading the listed words quickly and fluently with students. Underline the /ou/ sound in each word, say the /ou/ sound in the word, and then say the word. Repeat with each word and have students say the sounds and words with you. Invite students to think of sentences that contain *ow* and *ou* words with different pronunciations.

As a follow-up, have students complete the **Proud Crows and Owls reproducible (page 31)** to practice the letter patterns and pronunciations from the lesson.

Spelling the Sound /oi/

Two other spelling patterns that have the same pronunciation are *oi* and *oy*. They each make the sound /oi/. Encourage students to practice these spelling patterns and their pronunciation by completing the **A Choice Alien Voyage reproducible (page 32)**. Invite them to practice their fluency of *oi* and *oy* words by reading aloud the story to a partner. As students read the story, they will notice that words with these spelling patterns are boldface. Ask them to circle any words their partner pronounces incorrectly and go back to practice reading these words again.

Name _____ Date _____

Proud Crows and Owls

Directions: Say the words aloud. Listen to how they are pronounced. Write each word in the correct column according to the sound it makes.

/ou/			/ō/
	thrown	crowd	
	cloud	mound	
	pouch	gown	
	round	round	
	know	town	
	grow	loud	
	bowl	frown	
	owner	low	
	mow	shown	
	mouth	follow	
	crown	glow	
	growl	stow	
	shout	blow	
	howl	slow	
	down	count	
	flow	wound	
	proud	doubt	
	arrow	show	
	borrow	snow	
	yellow	known	

Name _____ Date _____

A Choice Alien Voyage

Directions: Read the passage aloud to a partner to practice your fluency with words that have *oi* and *oy* spelling patterns. As you read, have your partner circle the boldface words you do *not* read fluently. When you finish, practice writing and reading the circled words.

Roy's mother always said that his sister had the **poise** of a star. Not a movie star, but those you see glowing in the night sky, bright and always there. He felt lucky to be her brother, as it happened through no **choice** of his own.

It was summertime, and Susan was home from college for the first time after many months away. Something about her had changed. Now she was eating burgers made from **soybeans**. And her **voice** sounded strange when she talked on the telephone at night with a **boy**. Worst of all, she used to play with **Roy** and his **toys**, but now she rolled her eyes with **annoyance** and tried to **avoid** him.

Roy began to wonder if perhaps his sister was a **decoy**. Perhaps alien creatures had **destroyed** Susan and left this **joyless** copy in her place. He didn't like this new version at all. It could spend hours just lying about in the sun, **broiling** in the heat, as if life was just a boring **void**. He wondered if there was some spy's trick he could **employ** to bring his sister back, a remedy cure that would **poison** this impostor's body and **foil** the master alien plan.

He borrowed several books from the library that featured alien **voyages** from outer space, but none addressed this particular **point**. His mother noticed nothing unusual. But one day as she **toiled** in the **soil** of the garden, she looked up and said, "Susan, why don't you take **Roy** to the beach tomorrow. You can just as easily **boil** out there as here."

"But Mom . . ." Susan and **Roy joined** together in a wail. **Roy** did not know what new strangeness this could **deploy**, and Susan didn't want to **spoil** an entire day at the beach babysitting her little brother.

The tide stretched far out into a deep, **royal** blue of ocean, and the waves crashed in with a loud rumbling **noise**. **Roy** begged Susan to build sandcastles with him.

"No, let's walk," she said, and he followed her. Every now and then they stopped to watch the **rejoicing** seagulls. His sister stopped next to a tidepool and turned to **Roy** with a smile.

"Come look," she called, and he hurried over, **hoisting** himself up to gaze into the pool. **Coiled** into the nooks was a bright yellow starfish, shimmering in the water like a new **coin**.

"Wow, a real living star under the water," **Roy** said, and his sister laughed. For some reason that **Roy** couldn't quite explain, he knew his real sister was back.

Off-the-Wall Writing Waltz

The general spelling rule is that when the letter *a* follows *w*, the *a* usually makes the sound /ŏ/. However, there are exceptions to this rule. The letter *e* at the end of a word affects the vowel, so that the *a* is pronounced /ā/, as in *wade* and *wake*. The letter *r* also affects the vowel and causes it to be pronounced /ôr/, as in *warm* and *war*. The spelling pattern *ay* produces the /ā/ sound, as in *way*.

Linguistic Pattern

When the letter a follows w, it often makes the sound /ŏ/.

Write the following words on the board: *walrus, wallaby, waltz, walk, want, wand, water, watch.* Pronounce them with students, and stress the /ŏ/ sound. Have students drop their jaws and open their mouths as they enunciate the sound. Solicit other *wa* (/ŏ/) words from students and write them on the board.

Then write the following sentence on the board for pronunciation practice. Underline *wa* in the words that are pronounced with an /ŏ/ sound: *Walter the walrus watched the children wander through the aquarium while eating walnuts.*

Invite students to use the words they listed to write a ten-sentence story. Have them write the words at the top of a sheet of paper. Then ask students to write a sentence that contains one *wa* (/ŏ/) word. Tell them to underline that word in their sentence and cross it off the list at the top of the paper. Then tell students to exchange papers and get nine classmates to contribute to the story in the same manner. Inform them that they will be timed and you will give a signal when it's time to exchange papers. Remind the class that each new sentence must contain one *wa* (/ŏ/) word not used previously.

Signal to students that it is time to change writers by playing waltz music for 15 seconds (set a timer). Students must exchange papers within this time limit. Reset the timer for three minutes, during which students will read what has already been written and write a new sentence. Continue in this manner until all ten students have written a sentence. Remind the class that the last sentence should conclude the story.

While students read aloud their stories, listen and assess for fluency, prosody, and speed of decoding.

Soft *c* and Hard *c*

The consonant *c* has two sounds, soft *c* as in *cent* and hard *c* as in *can*. The soft *c*, or /s/ sound, occurs when the letters *e*, *i*, or *y* come after the letter *c*. The hard *c*, or /k/ sound, occurs when any other letters follow the letter *c*. To help students discover this linguistic pattern, use the following "Where Am I?" activity.

Where Am I?

Make a copy of the **"Where Am I?" Details reproducibles (pages 37–39)**. Cut apart the cards and distribute them to students. Have students check to make sure they understand all the words and are able to enunciate the sentences clearly. Point out that each sentence contains a boldface word or words with soft *c* and hard *c* sounds.

Have students walk around the room and shake hands with a classmate while reading aloud their sentences. Make sure everyone gets to share their cards with each other. Encourage students to listen for context clues to discern the topic of all the sentences.

After everyone has shared their sentences, have students return to their seats. Ask them to guess what all the sentences described and congratulate those students who guessed correctly that it was Antarctica. Collect the cards.

Encourage students to recall and write as many details about Antarctica as they can. If you wish, give the student with the most details a small prize.

Distribute the cards again and have students read the sentences at their seats. Tell students to read their sentences aloud to the class and then repeat the boldface word or words. Write those words on the board in columns, but do not label the columns. Write the words with *c* followed by *e*, *i*, or *y* in one column and the words with *c* followed by another letter in a second column. If a word contains two *c*'s and one is a hard *c* and the other is a soft *c* (e.g., *circus*), write that word in a third column.

After you have written all the words on the board, point to the top word in one of the columns. Pronounce the word, underline the letter *c* and the letter next to it, and say the word again. Ask the class what sound the letter *c* makes and say that sound. For example, if the word you are pointing to is *century*, say *century*. Underline the letters *ce*. Say *century* again, point to the underlined *ce*, and ask: *What sound does **ce** make?* Students should respond: */s/.*

When you have gone through all the words in this manner, ask students to tell you the pronunciation rule for the letter *c* linguistic pattern. They should come to the conclusion that when *c* is followed by *e*, *i*, or *ỵ*, it makes the */s/* sound. It is a soft *c*. Otherwise, it is a hard *c* and makes the */k/* sound. Help students with the terminology of hard *c* and soft *c*. Congratulate them on their self-discovery!

"Where Am I?" Word Lists

Words with Hard c			
academic	coastal	continent	discovered
accumulated	coastline	continental	expect
active	cold	continents	extraction
actually	coldest	continual	historic
became	combined	contradictions	indicate
because	come	converge	landscape
calendars	comes	cooperate	location
called	commercial	countries	locations
can	commission	courting	Mexico
carried	common	courtship	prospecting
claims	comparable	cover	recorded
clean	comparatively	covers	spectacular
climate	comparison	creatures	track
clock	cone	crowd	tropical
clocks	connection	cruise	vacation
clothes	conserving	cubic	volcano
coal	constitute	curious	volcanoes
coast	contains	current	volcanologists

Words with Soft c			
celebrate	cities	influence	scientists
center	December	once	since
Centigrade	distance	ounce	space
century	excess	percent	species
cereal	glaciers	place	
certify	ice	precipitation	
cinemas	icebergs	scenery	

Words with Hard c and Soft c		
accident	circles	scarcity
bicycle	circus	

As a follow-up to this activity, give students a copy of the **Reviewing Soft c and Hard c reproducible (page 40)**. Ask students to use what they learned to complete the reproducible.

"Where Am I?" Details

Don't worry if, by **accident**, you forget to bring your umbrella here on **vacation**. It is the driest **place** on Earth.	**Scientists certify** that the amount of **precipitation** here is **comparable** to that in the world's hot deserts.	The terrain here is 98 **percent** thick **continental ice** sheet and two **percent** barren rock.
Glaciers form **ice** shelves along about half of the **coastline**, while floating **ice** shelves **constitute** 11 **percent** of this **continent**.	You have to wear really warm **clothes** to visit this **place**. It is the **coldest**, highest, driest, windiest **location** on Earth!	The **distance** from one side to the other is vast. It is the fifth largest landmass on Earth: 5,400,000 square miles, as large as the United States and **Mexico combined**.
There are no **cinemas** with surround sound, but it is surrounded by three oceans.	The **ice**, which has **accumulated** over millions of years, is up to three miles deep and **covers** about 99 **percent** of the **continent**.	It is a **continent** of **contradictions**: **volcanoes** erupt from a frozen **landscape**; there are miles of snow and **ice**, yet hardly any snow falls each year.
The **ice** on this **continent** equals about six million **cubic** miles. If the **climate became tropical** and the **ice** melted, global sea levels would rise about 200 feet.	The **ice** here does not float on top of the ocean. It is a **continent because** there is land underneath the immense **ice cover**.	It only takes an **ounce** of knowledge to realize you don't need a bathing suit on this **vacation**. The average temperature is –49° **Centigrade**. Water temperature averages a **comparatively** balmy 33° Fahrenheit.

"Where Am I?" Details

The lowest temperature **recorded** anywhere on Earth was measured here at –128.6° Fahrenheit.	Rain rarely falls here because of the **cold** air temperatures. The **curious** have also **discovered** it rarely snows either; it gets less than six inches per year.	If you like sunshine, you **can celebrate** here; the sun shines 24 hours a day for six months every year. Just don't **expect** to get warm. The winds along the **coast** often reach 200 mph.
If the approximately 28 people who live in the government station want to eat **cereal**, it must be flown in. Otherwise, their only **connection** to the outside world is via the Internet, phone, and radio.	Much of what we know about this **continent** is gathered from **space**. Satellites **track** changes in water temperature, sea **ice cover**, and ozone layer shrinkage and expansion above the **continent**.	If you lived here, do you know to what time zone you would set your **clock**? **Actually**, all time zones **converge** on this **continent**, so residents have agreed to set their **clocks** to New Zealand time.
Plant and animal fossils and **coal** beds **indicate** that it was **once** warm here.	**Volcanologists** eagerly **crowd** the **cone** of its **active volcano**, which is 12,447 feet high, to monitor its **continual** small eruptions. The **volcano**, **called** Mt. Erebus, has a permanent lava lake in its **center**.	The western part of this **continent** has the potential for breaking up into giant **icebergs**.
The largest **current** in the world **circles** from west to east around this **continent**. It is the only **current** to sweep all the way around the world without being stopped by a landmass.	Is there oil and gas here? It's an **academic** question because oil **prospecting** and **extraction** was banned in 1991.	No **circus** ever **comes** here **because** there are no **cities** or states. People **can** only live on government bases or stations.

"Where Am I?" Details

Seven **countries** have **historic claims** to territory on this **continent**, but all of them have agreed to put their **claims** aside and **cooperate** with 36 other **countries** in studying and **conserving** the world benefits found here.

If you rode a **bicycle** here, you would not have to pedal. It is the windiest **place** on Earth. Winds flow down the **coastal** slopes under the **influence** of gravity, sometimes up to 327 kilometers per hour.

This **continent** is the highest on Earth; its average elevation is 2,300 meters (7,500 feet). In **comparison**, the average elevation of Australia is only 340 meters.

During the winter, this **continent** doubles in size **because** of the large amount of sea **ice** that forms at its periphery.

The general isolation of this **continent** has allowed it to avoid industrial pollution **common** to other **continents**, so snow and **ice** here are the purest in the world. The **ice contains** 90 **percent** of the world's fresh water.

Early 19th **century** explorers first visited this **place** to hunt whales and seals. By 1830, the fur seal was almost totally wiped out in many **locations**. **Commercial** sealing has not been **carried** out here **since** the 1950s.

The story of whaling here is one of greed and **excess**. First, one **species** was hunted to **scarcity**, then the next, and so on. The International Whaling **Commission** (IWC) did not suspend **commercial** whaling until 1986.

It's a **circus** every summer when tourists **come** to visit aboard approximately 20 different **cruise** vessels. Weather and **ice**, not **clocks** and **calendars**, set the schedules for their journey.

November and early **December** is the **courting** season for penguins and seabirds, and you **can** see their **spectacular courtship** rituals. Many elephant and fur seals are establishing their breeding territories as well.

In early **December**, the winter pack **ice** is starting to melt and break up. The **scenery** is white, **clean**, and pristine with pack **ice** and giant **icebergs**.

The most prominent inhabitant here is the penguin. However, other living **creatures** abound in the surrounding oceans. Many whales, six **species** of seals, and about 12 **species** of birds live and breed here.

Reviewing Soft c and Hard c

Directions: When the letter *c* is followed by *e*, *i*, or, *y*, it makes the sound */s/*, as in *center* (soft *c*). When it is followed by any other letter, it makes the sound */k/*, as in *can* (hard *c*). Write the correct answers on the lines below.

	What letter comes after *c*?	**Does *c* have the soft or hard sound?**
1. collect		
2. car		
3. climate		
4. dance		
5. construct		
6. curious		
7. coast		
8. city		
9. evidence		
10. microscope		
11. cereal		
12. citrus		
13. moccasins		
14. cylinder		
15. ceramic		
16. scratched		
17. cinch		
18. ounce		

Soft *g* and Hard *g*

Like the letter *c*, the consonant *g* also has two sounds, although the soft *g* sound is not as predictable as the soft *c* sound. The letter *g* usually makes the /j/ sound (as in *gem*) when it is followed by the vowels *e*, *i*, or *y*. It is called *soft g*. However, even when the vowels *e*, *i*, or *y* follow the *g*, it is sometimes pronounced /g/ (as in *give* and *get*). Then it is called *hard g*. The letter *g* makes the hard /g/ sound (as in *garden*) when it is followed by any other letter. To help students discover this linguistic pattern, use the following "Where Am I Now?" activity.

Linguistic Patterns

g usually = /j/ when followed by *e*, *i*, or *y*

g = /g/ when followed by all other letters, and occasionally *e*, *i*, or *y*

Where Am I Now?

Make a copy of the **"Where Am I Now?" Details reproducibles (pages 44–46)**. Cut apart the cards and distribute them to students. Have students check to make sure they understand all the words and are able to enunciate the sentences clearly. Point out that each sentence contains a boldface word or words containing soft *g* or hard *g* pronunciations.

Have students walk around the room and shake hands with a classmate while reading their sentences aloud. Make sure everyone gets to share their cards with each other. Encourage students to listen for context clues to discern the topic of all the sentences.

After everyone has shared their sentences, have students return to their seats. Ask them to guess what all the sentences described and congratulate those students who guessed correctly that it was Nepal. Collect the cards.

Have students recall and write as many details about Nepal as they can. If you wish, give the student with the most details a small prize.

Distribute the cards again and have students read the sentences at their seats. Tell students to read their sentences aloud to the class and then repeat the boldface words. Write those words on the board in specific columns, but do not label the columns. Write the words with *g* followed by *e*, *i*, or *y* in one column and words with *g* followed by any other letter in the second column.

After you have written all the words on the board, point to the top word in one of the columns. Pronounce the word, underline the letter *g* and the letter next to it, and say the word again. Ask the class what sound the letter *g* makes and say that sound, either /j/ or /g/. For example, if the word you are pointing to is *generally*, say *generally*. Underline the letters *ge*. Say *generally* again, point to the underlined *ge*, and ask: *What sound does* **g** *make?* Students should respond: /j/.

When you have gone through all the words in this manner, ask students to tell you the pronunciation rule for the letter *g*. They should come to the conclusion that when *g* is followed by *e*, *i*, or *y*, it usually makes the /j/ sound, and it is a soft *g*. When the letter *g* is followed by any other letters, and sometimes *e*, *i*, or *y*, it is a hard *g* and makes the /g/ sound. Help students with the terminology of hard *g* and soft *g*. Congratulate them on their self-discovery!

As a follow-up to the activity, invite students to review what they learned. Give students a copy of the **Reviewing Soft *g* and Hard *g* reproducible (page 47)**. Invite them to complete the reproducible individually or with a partner.

"Where Am I Now?" Word Lists

Soft *g* Words (Followed by *e*, *i*, or *y*)	
age	giant
Ages	gorgeous**
allergies	huge
changeover	imagination
courage	imagine
emergency	legend
encourage	legendary
endangered	magic
exchange	oxygen
general	range
generally	religion
generous	tiger*
geography**	tigers*
get*	village

Hard *g* Words	
began	golden
beggars	gone
Bengal	good
dogs	gorgeous**
enigmatic	governor
flag	granted
flags	great
gate	greatest
gathered	green
gave	groups
geography**	guide
ghastly	magnificent
glaring	non-rectangular
go	triangle
goats	triangles

* These words are exceptions. They have the hard *g* /g/ sound.

** These words include both the hard *g* /g/ and soft *g* /j/ sounds.

It tugs at our **imagination** because of its scenic splendor and cultural treasures.

Go when you are in **good** shape because it has some of the **greatest** hiking trails on Earth. It sits on the Himalayan mountain **range**.

May and early June are **generally** too hot and dusty for comfortable traveling.

When you are planning your trip, consider **geography** and weather. From mid-June to September, monsoons can obscure mountain views with clouds and turn hiking trails into mud.

You might feel like you are on a **magic** carpet ride when you travel here.

During your visit to this **enigmatic** place, you might feel like you have stepped into a time machine and **gone** back in history.

The first recorded history here in the 7th–8th century BC told of sheep, not **goats**, and a fondness for knives.

This place experienced a **golden age** of art and architecture between 200–800 AD.

Here in 879 AD, a period known as the Dark **Ages began**.

The main **religion**, Hinduism, and the caste system were re-imposed in 200 AD and still continue today.

For hundreds of years, its army seemed unstoppable and became **legendary** because of their **courage**.

One ruler seized control by carrying out a **ghastly** massacre and butchered several hundred of the most important men while they **gathered** in a courtyard.

The **huge** palaces in this place are **gorgeous**.	For over 100 years, its previously **generous** borders were sealed to anyone wanting to **get** in.	In 1846, the **governor gave** himself the title *Rama*, proclaimed himself prime minister for life, and made the office hereditary.
It was a country surrounded by myth and **legend** until after WWII, because no foreigner could enter.	The first outsider **granted** entrance to this place in over 100 years was a Swiss explorer in 1951.	Today the **glaring** reality is that this country is among the poorest and least developed in the world, with almost one-third of its population living below the poverty line.
In May 1991, the attempt for a **changeover** to democracy proceeded in an orderly fashion.	Since 1991, democracy has not worked. In February 2005, the ruling king declared a state of **emergency** because of the opposition to his rule.	In 2007, its citizens were hopeful that the upcoming **general** elections would provide peace and stability in their country.
Dozens of different tribal **groups** live here.	Its **flag** is one of only two **non-rectangular flags** in the world. It is two overlapping red **triangles** with a blue border. The lower **triangle** shows a white, 12-pointed sun.	A special festival in November called *Tihar* honors crows, **dogs**, and cows.

"Where Am I Now?" Details

If you fly here, you will not **get** lost at the wrong **gate**. There is only one small international airport.	In a plane, you may **get** a **great** view of the Himalayan mountain **range**.	**Go** to the bank before you leave and **exchange** your dollars for rupees.
Imagine a perfect snow-capped mountain. **Imagine** a calm lake reflecting that mountain. Now **imagine** a **village** on the shore and shops selling prayer **flags**.	This place is close to towering, snow-capped mountains. They look **magnificent**.	Here you can hire a **guide** to see crocodiles, rhinos, sloth bears, and **tigers**.
Tourists who have visited this country **encourage** others to experience its beauty and charm.	Take a deep breath of **oxygen** before you come here because the **great** elevation might leave you breathless.	As in many capital cities, there are **beggars** on the streets. But you may be surprised to see monkeys as well!
If you have **allergies**, do not come here between February and April. That is when **giant** wildflowers are in bloom.	The best time to visit is at the start of the dry season in October and November. The countryside is lush and **green** following the monsoon period.	The royal **Bengal tiger** is one of the **endangered** species that lives here.

Reviewing Soft g and Hard g

Directions: When the letter g is followed by e, i, or y, it makes the sound /j/, as in gem (soft g). But sometimes when g is followed by e, i, or y, it can make the the sound /g/, as in give and get (hard g). When g is followed by any other letter, it makes the sound /g/, as in garden. Write the correct answers on the lines below.

	What letter comes after g?	Does g have the soft or hard sound?
1. grand		
2. great		
3. ago		
4. gate		
5. goblet		
6. giant		
7. gypsy		
8. germ		
9. oxygen		
10. giraffe		
11. geyser		
12. gyoza		
13. girl		
14. giggle		
15. gearshift		
16. goal		
17. gentle		
18. geese		

Flip-Chart Books

Have students create individual flip-chart books as you progress through the linguistics activities. You may wish to have students make one book for each linguistic pattern (e.g., one flip-chart book may be titled *ow and ou*). Each book should contain various spelling patterns, the sounds the spelling patterns make, and stories students write to practice the target words. These small references are extremely handy for students to keep at their desks or in their binders.

The first time you have students make a book, you may wish to make a transparency copy of the directions below so you can display them as you demonstrate each step.

1. Choose two pieces of different-colored paper. Stack them so the colors alternate. Fold the papers in half, lengthwise. Then unfold the papers and cut along each fold, one at a time.

2. Put one stack of half-sheets on top of the other, making sure that the colors alternate. Cut diagonally along the short top and bottom edges so they come to a point, creating a "V" design. You may also wish to scallop the "V" design to make your book unique.

3. Now arrange the papers so that each sheet shows under the next by approximately 1/4". Then fold over the upper portion of the stack so that all eight pages are exposed.

4. Staple the flip-chart book across the top three times to hold the pages in place.

5. The flip-chart book has a cover page and seven pages to write on. Write the title of the book or a table of contents on the cover page. Then write labels on the exposed flaps to indicate linguistic patterns contained in the book.

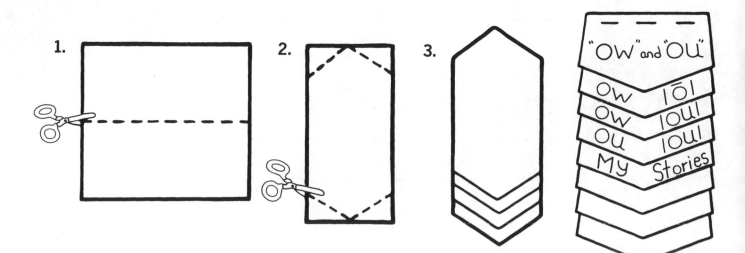

978-1-4129-5825-7

Understanding Pronunciation Patterns

Invite students to play "Understanding Pronunciation Patterns" to practice the following linguistics patterns: *ai, oa, oo,* and *ow.* Students will use what they have learned to read nonsense words, pronounce words with specific spelling patterns, answer riddles, and identify consonant pairs.

Make a copy of the **Understanding Pronunciation Patterns Game Cards reproducible (page 51)**. Cut apart the boxes and glue each box to an index card. Arrange the cards in point order (smallest to largest) with their respective headings.

Draw a large 5 x 5 grid on the board. Label the columns and the point values, as shown in the diagram below.

Nonsense Words with *ai* and *oa*	Words with *oo*	Words with *ow*	Definitions of *oa* Words	Consonant Pairs
100	100	100	100	100
200	200	200	200	200
300	300	300	300	300
400	400	400	400	400
500	500	500	500	500

Divide the class into two teams and give each team a name. Explain to the teams that they will take turns choosing a category and a point value. For example, a team member might say: *Words with* **oo** *for 300 points.* Describe each category for students as follows:

Nonsense Words with *ai* and *oa*—*Words in this category follow the pronunciation patterns for* **oa** *and* **ai***. You must pronounce these nonsense words correctly.*

Words with *oo*—*Words in this category are spelled with two* **o***'s. You must pronounce these words correctly, knowing which words have an /o͞o/ sound and which have an /o͝o/ sound.*

Words with *ow*—*Words in this category are spelled with* **ow***. You must pronounce these words correctly, knowing which words have an /ō/ sound and which have an /ou/ sound.*

Definitions of *oa* Words—*Words in this category all contain the letter pattern **oa**, pronounced /ō/, as in **boat**. I will read you a definition, and you must guess the **oa** word that is being described.*

Consonant Pairs—*You must learn which consonants are made with the same mouth positions as other consonants. For this category, I will show you a consonant, and you must tell me what consonant is its consonant pair.*

After students choose a category and point value, give them the corresponding game card to read or answer. Have students read the words silently first, so when they read the words aloud, they read them correctly. Record teams' points when they answer correctly and draw an X over the corresponding box. (All the words must be pronounced correctly for points to be awarded.)

Alternate turns between teams. If a team member answers or reads the words incorrectly, a member of the other team may have a chance to answer or read the card correctly for the points. Regardless of whether or not that player earns points, another player from the same team may choose a category and point value for a new turn.

When all the categories have been read or answered, the team with the most points wins!

Nonsense Words with *ai* and *oa*	Words with *oo*	Words with *ow*	Definitions of *oa* Words	Consonant Pairs
100	100	100	100	100
200	200	200	200	200
300	300	300	300	300
		400	400	400
	500	500	500	500

Bread that is heated and browned—toast!

Understanding Pronunciation Patterns Game Cards

Nonsense Words with *ai* and *oa*	Words with *oo*	Words with *ow*	Definitions of *oa* Words	Consonant Pairs
100 raiboatoa	**100** ŏŏ, ōō, ōŏ, ŏŏ	**100** down, thrown, clown	**100** something flat on which you drive	**100** p
200 goanaisai	**200** hook, ooze, cookie, tooth	**200** lower, shower, coward, how	**200** bread that is heated and browned	**200** g, d
300 maibaidoafai	**300** shook, brook, loose, zoom, hood	**300** blown, brown, thrown, brow	**300** land-dwelling amphibian with rough, wart-covered skin	**300** z, v, b
400 skainaitoadoa	**400** shoo, snoop, shook, nook, booth, wool	**400** dowdy, stow, tow, wow, glow	**400** to make thoroughly wet	**400** f, s, k, t
500 poafaidoalairaigoa	**500** rookie, goof, boot, cook, hoot, soot	**500** vow, dower, owe, cowlick, bowl	**500** to remain suspended on fluid without sinking	**500** d, p, g, z, v

Mastering Pronunciation Patterns

Invite students to play "Mastering Pronunciation Patterns" to practice the following linguistics patterns: *ch*, *ed*, *ea*, and *c* followed by *e*, *i*, or *y*. Students will use what they have learned to fluently read sentences that contain heteronyms and words with specific spelling patterns.

Make a copy of the **Mastering Pronunciation Patterns Game Cards reproducibles (pages 54–55)**. Cut apart the boxes and glue each box to an index card. Arrange the cards in point order (smallest to largest) with their respective headings.

Draw a large 5 x 5 grid on the board. Label the columns and the point values, as shown in the diagram below.

Heteronyms	Words with *ch*	Words with *ed*	Words with *ea*	Words with *c* Followed by *e, i,* or *y*
200	200	200	200	200
400	400	400	400	400
600	600	600	600	600
800	800	800	800	800
1,000	1,000	1,000	1,000	1,000

Divide the class into two teams and give each team a name. Explain to the teams that they will take turns choosing a category and a point value. For example, a team member might say: *Heteronyms for 600 points*. Describe each category for students as follows:

Heteronyms—*Each sentence in this category contains words that are heteronyms, words that are spelled the same but have different meanings and pronunciations.*

Words with *ch*—*Each sentence in this category contains words that have the spelling pattern **ch**. Remember as you read these words that **ch** has three different pronunciations.*

Words with *ed*—*Each sentence in this category contains words that have the spelling pattern **ed**. Remember as you read these words that **ed** has three different pronunciations.*

Words with ea—*Each sentence in this category contains words that have the spelling pattern* **ea**. *Remember as you read these words that* **ea** *has two different pronunciations.*

Words with c Followed by e, i, or y—*Each sentence in this category contains words spelled with a* **c**. *Remember as you read these words how their pronunciations change when* **e**, **i**, *or* **y** *comes after the letter* **c**.

After students choose a category and point value, give them the corresponding game card to read. Have students read the words silently first, so when they read the words aloud, they read them correctly. Record teams' points when they read the words fluently and draw an *X* over the corresponding box. All the words within the indicated category must be pronounced correctly for points to be awarded. For example, if a student reads the sentence in the category *Heteronyms* for 400 points, he or she earns all the points if the heteronyms *moped* (motorized bicycle) and *moped* (sulked) are pronounced correctly.

Alternate turns between teams. If a team member reads the words incorrectly, a member of the other team may have a chance to read the card correctly for the points. Regardless of whether or not that player earns points, another player from the same team may choose a category and point value for a new turn.

When all the categories have been read or answered, the team with the most points wins!

Mastering Pronunciation Patterns Game Cards

Heteronyms	Words with *ch*	Words with *ed*	Words with *ea*	Words with *c* Followed by *e*, *i*, or *y*
200 The drawer kept her drawings in the bottom drawer of the china cabinet.	**200** The coach was speechless after the enchanting performance by the school chorus.	**200** Mia looked surprised as she squatted and smelled the flower but discovered a bug.	**200** I had a dream that beneath the sea a heavy treasure was concealed.	**200** Did you notice the curved surface of the bicycle's seat that the clown in the center was riding?
400 He rode his moped close to the door, read that the office was closed, and moped away.	**400** The scholars drove their Chevy to the ranch, not the beach, to search for peaches.	**400** They clapped, jumped, and cheered when he graduated and walked the stage.	**400** After a breakfast of beans and bread, I was ready to watch the eagles spread their feathers.	**400** The magnificent palace was recently discovered and celebrated as an architectural site.
600 The principal had to intermediate between the arguing intermediate students and told them to stop their row and line up in a row.	**600** The chauvinistic bachelor saw a fuchsia-colored brochure in the chiropractor's office that advertised chocolate enchiladas.	**600** As Lisa worked and picked the strawberries, she decided when she was finished that she wanted to eat the biggest one.	**600** The man's endeavor to become wealthy in trade failed because he dealt in cheap leather.	**600** Evidence has surfaced that calling on your cell phone while driving can cause a traffic accident or a costly collision.

Words with c Followed by e, i, or y

800

The century-old Cyclops sat comfortably on a cylinder in the tropical climate under the cirrus clouds watching a centipede circling around the cylinder's circumference.

1,000

A large percentage of customers rode the escalator to the cinema to watch a comedy about health-conscious, concerned citizens who wore moccasins and danced around spruce trees to improve circulation.

Words with ea

800

After he was beat in the race, the sweaty, out-of-breath contestant took a seat to clear his head.

1,000

The easy hike from the beach near the stream lead to a nearby mountain peak where we saw a weasel.

Words with ed

800

When the U.S. sprinter crossed the finish line, the crowd blinked, stared at the replay, nodded their approval, and applauded the gold-medal performance.

1,000

The coach hoped that the players listened and were interested as he showed them how to throw a ball so that it curved right before the batter swung and missed the pitch.

Words with ch

800

The chauffeur was quite a character and insisted all his passengers munch on chocolate and cheese for lunch under a chandelier, which often gave them a bellyache.

1,000

The research student presented his chemistry speech that won him a scholarship on "The Effects of Chlorine" at a conference in Cheyenne, Wyoming.

Heteronyms

800

I objected to sitting so near to the fountain when a dove dove after a shiny object in the water.

1,000

He resented the fact that the e-mail was resent in error, since he had already stated that he was content with the content of the manuscript.

Heteronyms

Heteronym Partners

Heteronyms are words that are spelled the same but have different pronunciations and meanings. Some heteronyms have completely different pronunciations and meanings (e.g., the noun *row* /rou/, meaning *fight*; the verb *row* /rō/, meaning *to paddle*). Other heteronyms are similar in meaning when the accent changes from one syllable to another and their parts of speech are related, as in a noun to a verb (e.g., the noun *conflict* /**kŏn'**-flĭkt/, meaning *disagreement or fight;* the verb *conflict* /kən-**flĭkt'**/, meaning *to be in opposition, to differ.*

To introduce heteronyms, write the following words on the board: *row, conflict, bass, bow, close, live.* Do not write their pronunciations or meanings. Ask students if they know the pronunciations and meanings of the words. Students should shortly discover that each word has two different pronunciations and sometimes several different meanings.

Refer to the **Heteronyms List 1** and **Heteronyms List 2 reproducibles (pages 57–58)** and write the meaning for one heteronym on an index card for each student. Make sure that for each meaning you write, you also write the meaning for the corresponding heteronym. Then copy a class set of both Heteronyms List reproducibles. Give copies to each student to use as references.

Pass out the index cards to students in random order. When all students have a card, tell them to find their heteronym partner. Students must figure out what their heteronym is by reading its meaning. Then they must find the classmate who holds the card with the corresponding heteronym. After all partners are paired together, have students read the meaning on their index card, say the heteronym, and then spell it. For example, pairs of students might respond in the following manner:

Student 1: *A knot with two or more loops is a **bow**, spelled **b-o-w**.*

Student 2: *To bend the head in greeting means to **bow**, also spelled **b-o-w**.*

Note that the pronunciation of each heteronym is different, even though the words are spelled the same. The meaning of each heteronym is different as well.

Collect all the index cards so they can be redistributed among students to repeat the same activity. Save the cards to use in the game *"Heteronym Memory Match"* (page 60).

Heteronyms List 1

Directions: Notice how the pronunciations of these heteronyms change in different places and do not depend on where the accent occurs.

agape: /ə-**gāp'**/ *(adj)* wide open; /ä-**gä'**-pā/ *(n)* form of love

appropriate: /ə-**prō'**-prē-ĭt/ *(adj)* proper or correct; /ə-**prō'**-prē-āt/ *(v)* to take possession of

bass: /băs/ *(n)* type of fish; /bās/ *(n)* low pitch

bow: /bō/ *(n)* knot with two or more loops sometimes used for decoration; weapon used to shoot arrows; rod used to play a musical instrument; /bou/ *(v)* to bend the head in greeting; *(n)* front of a ship

close: /klōs/ *(adj)* near in space or time; /klōz/ *(v)* to shut; to make unavailable for use

deliberate: /dĭ-**lĭb'**-ər-ĭt/ *(adj)* intentional; /dĭ-**lĭb'**-ə-rāt/ *(v)* to think about carefully

does: /dŭz/ *(v)* form of the verb *do*; /dōz/ *(n)* plural of *doe* (female deer)

dove: /dŭv/ *(n)* bird; /dōv/ *(v)* past tense of verb *to dive*

drawer: /drôr/ *(n)* boxlike compartment that is opened by pulling out; /**drô'**-ər/ *(n)* person who draws

excuse: /ĭk-**skyōōz'**/ *(v)* to forgive or overlook; /ĭk-**skyōōs'**/ *(n)* explanation to justify excusing

intermediate: /ĭn-tər-**mē'**-dē-ĭt/ *(adj)* between; /ĭn-tər-mē-dē-**āt'**/ *(v)* to intervene

lead: /lēd/ *(v)* to guide; /lĕd/ *(n)* metallic element

live: /līv/ *(adj)* having life; /lĭv/ *(v)* to be alive or exist

moped: /**mō'**-pĕd/ *(n)* motorized bicycle; /mōpt/ *(v)* acted gloomy or dejected

number: /**nŭm'**-bər/ *(n)* symbol used in counting; /**nŭm'**-ər/ *(adj)* more numb

predicate: /**prĕd'**-ĭ-kĭt/ *(n)* part of a sentence; /**prĕd'**-ĭ-kāt/ *(v)* to imply; assert or declare

resent: /rĭ-**zĕnt'**/ *(v)* to be indignant; /**rē'**-**sĕnt'**/ *(v)* sent again

resort: /rĭ-**zôrt'**/ *(n)* vacation spot; *(v)* to have recourse; /**rē'**-**sôrt'**/ *(v)* to sort again

resume: /**rĕz'**-ŏŏ-mā/ *(n)* document listing professional experience; /rĭ-**zōōm'**/ *(v)* to restart

row: /rō/ *(v)* to propel a boat with oars; *(n)* line of objects; /rou/ *(n)* fight

sewer: /**sō'**-ər/ *(n)* person who sews; /**sōō'**-ər/ *(n)* underground channel for sewage or rainwater

sow: /sō/ *(v)* to plant seeds; /sou/ *(n)* adult female hog or bear

tear: /tîr/ *(n)* clear, salty liquid from the eyes; /târ/ *(v)* to rip

tier: /tîr/ *(n)* row or rank; /**tī'**-ər/ *(n)* one who ties

tower: /**tou'**-ər/ *(n)* tall building; /**tō'**-ər/ *(n)* one who tows

wind: /wĭnd/ *(n)* moving air; /wīnd/ *(v)* to wrap around

wound: /wōōnd/ *(n)* injury; /wound/ *(v)* past tense of verb *wind*

Heteronyms List 2

Directions: Notice how the pronunciations of these heteronyms change when the accented syllables change.

affect: /ə-**fĕkt'**/ (v) to change or influence; /**ăf'**-ĕkt/ (n) feeling or emotion

attribute: /ə-**trĭb'**-yo͞ot/ (v) to relate to a cause; /**ăt'**-rə-byo͞ot/ (n) characteristic

conduct: /kən-**dŭkt'**/ (v) to direct; to manage or control; /**kŏn'**-dŭkt/ (n) behavior or actions

conflict: /kən-**flĭkt'**/ (v) to be in opposition; to differ; /**kŏn'**-flĭkt/ (n) disagreement or fight

console: /kən-**sōl'**/ (v) to give comfort; /**kŏn'**-sōl/ (n) floor cabinet; desk-like part of an organ that contains the keyboard, stops, and pedals; storage compartment between bucket seats in an automobile

content: /kən-**tĕnt'**/ (adj) satisfied; /**kŏn'**-tĕnt/ (n) meaningful part

contest: /kən-**tĕst'**/ (v) to dispute; / **kŏn'**-tĕst/ (n) competition

contract: /kən-**trăkt'**/ (v) to shrink; to enter into a formal agreement; /**kŏn'**-trăkt/ (n) formal agreement

converse: /kən-**vûrs'**/ (v) to talk; /**kŏn'**-vûrs/ (n) opposite

convert: /kən-**vûrt'**/ (v) to change into another form; to change one's belief; /**kŏn'**-vûrt/ (n) one whose belief was changed

convict: /kən-**vĭkt'**/ (v) to prove guilty; /**kŏn'**-vĭkt/ (n) prisoner

desert: /dĭ-**zûrt'**/ (v) to leave; abandon; /**dĕz'**-ərt/ (n) barren or desolate arid area

entrance: /ĕn-**trăns'**/ (v) to fill with wonder; /**ĕn'**-trəns/ (n) passage by which to enter

incense: /ĭn-**sĕns'**/ (v) to anger or infuriate; /**ĭn'**-sĕns/ (n) substance burned to produce a pleasant odor

intern: /ĭn-**tûrn'**/ (v) to confine to a certain area; /**ĭn'**-tûrn/ (n) person in supervised training

invalid: /ĭn-**văl'**-ĭd/ (adj) not legally valid; /**ĭn'**-və-lĭd/ (n) person who is sick or incapacitated

minute: /mī-**no͞ot'**/ (adj) very small; /**mĭn'**-ĭt/ (n) sixty seconds

moderate: /mŏd-ər-**āt'**/ (v) to preside over; /**mŏd'**-ər-ĭt/ (adj) not excessive or extreme

object: /əb-**jĕct'**/ (v) to protest; /**ŏb'**-jĭkt/ (n) thing

perfect: /pər-**fĕkt'**/ (v) to make flawless; /**pûr'**-fĭkt/ (adj) flawless

permit: /pər-**mĭt'**/ (v) to allow; /**pûr'**-mĭt/ (n) document giving permission

present: /prĭ-**zĕnt'**/ (v) to introduce; /**prĕz'**-ənt/ (n) gift

produce: /prə-**do͞os'**/(v) to bring forth or manufacture; /**prō'**-do͞os/ (n) vegetables

rebel: /rĭ-**bĕl'**/ (v) to refuse allegiance or defy authority; /**rĕb'**-əl/ (n) one who refuses allegiance or defies authority

refuse: /rĭ-**fyo͞oz'**/ (v) to decline to do; /**rĕf'**-yo͞os/ (n) trash or rubbish

subject: /səb-**jĕkt'**/ (v) to force upon; /**sŭb'**-jĕkt/ (n) the theme; course or area of study; one who is under the rule of another

suspect: /sə-**spĕkt'**/ (v) to have suspicion; /**sŭs'**-pĕkt/ (n) one suspected of a crime

Both Words Count

Refer to Heteronyms Lists 1 and 2 (pages 57–58). Write the heteronyms on separate slips of paper and place the words in a paper bag. If you have more students in your class than heteronyms, include some of the words twice (you should have enough heteronyms so each student gets three). Then give each student three index cards. Ask students to draw three heteronyms from the bag. Have them write three different sentences (one on each index card). Each sentence must contain at least two meanings and two pronunciations of the heteronyms. Tell students to underline the heteronyms in their sentences. For example, a student who draws *bass*, *dove*, and *wound* from the bag might write the following sentences on separate index cards:

- *There was a <u>bass</u> painted on his big <u>bass</u> drum.*

- *At the sound of the gunshot, the <u>dove</u> <u>dove</u> out of the bushes.*

- *The nurse <u>wound</u> the bandage around his <u>wound</u>.*

Collect the sentence cards and shuffle them in random order. Divide the class into two teams. Have students from each team draw a sentence card, one at a time. If students can read the sentence and correctly pronounce each heteronym and all the other words correctly, their team gets five points. Show each index card to the class so they can see the words. Continue playing until all the sentence cards have been read. The team with the most points wins.

Heteronym Memory Match

Reinforce students' understanding and recall of heteronyms with this simple matching game. If students do not have them, copy class sets of the Heteronyms Lists 1 and 2 (pages 57–58) for students to use as references during the game.

Choose 12 pairs of heteronym meaning cards your class created in the "Heteronym Partners" activity (page 56). Tape the cards onto the board so students can read the meanings. Arrange the cards in four rows and six columns. Use a broad-tipped marker to write the numbers 1–24 on blank index cards. Tape these cards on top of the heteronym meanings, so students can only see the numbers.

Divide the class into two teams. Ask a player to choose two numbers. As a number is called, lift the corresponding card to reveal the heteronym meaning underneath. Challenge the class to guess the heteronym. Repeat the steps to reveal the second heteronym meaning. If the player has not found a heteronym pair, have a player from the other team say two numbers and repeat the steps. Encourage students to concentrate and try to remember which meanings are under which numbers. When a player successfully matches a heteronym pair, pull those cards off the board and give them to the appropriate team. Continue playing until all the heteronym pairs have been matched.

For additional practice with heteronyms, give students a copy of **The Nature of Nature reproducible (page 62)**. Invite them to read aloud the passage to a partner and listen for and circle all the heteronyms.

Only the Spelling Is the Same

Directions: Match the dictionary pronunciation with its meaning. Then write the heteronym.

1. /wīnd/ _____ symbol used in counting _____

2. /prə-**doos'**/ _____ bird _____

3. /**nŭm'**-ər/ _____ vegetables _____

4. /klōs/ _____ moving air _____

5. /sou/ _____ adult female hog or bear _____

6. /**nŭm'**-bər/ _____ to leave or abandon _____

7. /mī-**noot'**/ _____ to shut _____

8. /**ăf'**-ĕkt/ _____ to wrap around _____

9. /dĭ-**zŭrt'**/ _____ one who refuses allegiance or defies authority _____

10. /dōv/ _____ to bring forth or manufacture _____

11. /**rĕb'**-əl/ _____ barren or desolate arid area _____

12. /**dĕz'**-ərt/ _____ to plant seeds _____

13. /wĭnd/ _____ feeling or emotion _____

14. /**prō'**-doos/ _____ sixty seconds _____

15. /**mĭn'**-ĭt/ _____ past tense of verb *to dive* _____

16. /rĭ- **bĕl'**/ _____ more numb _____

17. /klōz/ _____ to change or influence _____

18. /dŭv/ _____ very small _____

19. /sō/ _____ near in space or time _____

20. /ə-**fĕkt'**/ _____ to refuse allegiance or deny authority _____

The Nature of Nature

Directions: Read the story aloud to a partner. Circle the words that are heteronyms.

At the entrance to the national park, Brent went to produce his Golden Eagle Pass and realized it was invalid. He decided to pay for a one-time entry permit instead of buying another annual pass. The drive through the desert had been long, though spectacular, as many cacti were in bloom, and he was not going to turn back now.

Immediately upon entering the park, the red rock formations loomed large in front of his car. Row after row of red towers stood at attention like soldiers refusing to bow. Brent could not tear his eyes away, and he refused to drive any faster. Although his car was in the lead, a young girl on a moped was now following close behind and would soon close the gap between their vehicles. She would have to excuse his slow pace. He had reached the object of his destination, and he was not going to be rushed, even if she objected.

Brent's car wound around and through the formations. The magnificent towers of the canyon caused him to feel more minute every minute. The smallness he felt, however, seemed to console him and take away all the conflict he sometimes felt. Content at last, he pulled into the Queen's Garden, ready for a moderate hike. Looking at the content of the map Brent had been presented at the gate, he decided to permit himself to tackle the two-mile hike called the Navajo Loop Trail. He would resort to taking pictures with his memory, as he had forgotten his camera. The real delight was his ability to converse with nature. Later in life, if Brent ever became an invalid, he would cherish these moments.

The wind whistled gently through his hair. Birds deliberately caught the currents and dove past him against the blue sky. The brilliant red towers of the canyon made this the most picturesque park he had ever visited. The spiral limestone formations resembled cathedrals, goblins with their mouths agape, and the tops of fairy castles. Brent would not need an excuse to return; this was reason enough. The attributes of the canyon had completely entranced him. Bryce Canyon National Park had just become his number one perfect resort.

Root Words and Roots

Many English words are formed by taking basic words and adding combinations of prefixes and suffixes to them. A basic word to which affixes (prefixes and suffixes) are added is called a *root word* because it forms the basis of a new word. The root word is also a word in its own right. For example, the word *lovely* consists of the root word *love* and the suffix *-ly*.

In contrast, a *root* is the basis of a new word, but it does not typically form a stand-alone word of its own. For example, the word *reject* is made up of the prefix *re-* and the Latin root *ject*, which is not a stand-alone word.

Guess the Meaning

Write the following words on the board: *running*, *hopeful*, *pretest*, *replay*, *walked*, *eating*, *worker*, *drinkable*, *happiest*, *gladly*, *scary*, *dissatisfy*, *thinking*. Have students identify the root words and underline them. Then have students think of additional words to add to the list. Ask them to underline those root words.

Then write the these words on the board: *judicial*, *aquarium*, *disrupt*, *maternal*. Tell students that each of these words contains a Latin root. Challenge the class to identify the root in each word and guess its meaning. You may wish to give students a hint by underlining the Latin root. The meanings of the roots are as follows: *jud*—to judge, *aqua*—water, *rupt*—to break, and *mater*—mother.

Ask students to explain the difference between root words and roots. Tell them that they are going to learn many Greek and Latin roots, which will help them become better readers. Stress to students that they can often figure out the meaning of an unfamiliar word if they recognize Greek and Latin roots and remember their meanings. This allows them to break the word into small *morphemes,* which give clues to the meaning of the entire word.

Allow students to practice working with root words and roots. Give them a copy of the **Mister Rojo** and **Roots and Beyond reproducibles (pages 64–65)**. Encourage students to complete the reproducibles individually or in pairs. Remind them that memorizing root words and roots will help them to decode words and read more fluently.

Mister Rojo

Directions: Read the story. Then write the boldface words and their root words on the lines.

It was a warm summer day. The sun was **shining brightly**. Alicia's red hair **glistened** as she **skipped** toward the car. Her **parents hurried** behind her. **Excitement filled** the air. Alicia had always wanted a puppy, and **finally** the day had **arrived**.

As she **entered** the pet shop, the **barking** of all the **dogs** was overwhelming. She didn't know which way to look first. Then she **noticed** a puppy with big brown **eyes** and red hair just like hers. Alicia knew **immediately** that this puppy was meant for her. As she held her new puppy **carefully** in her arms, he **gently** licked her chin. Alicia knew she would not have anymore **unhappy** days **wishing** for a puppy. She could feel his tail **wagging** back and forth. **Grinning broadly** from ear to ear, she told her parents, "I'm **going** to name him Mister Rojo."

Boldface Word	Root Word	Boldface Word	Root Word
1.		13.	
2.		14.	
3.		15.	
4.		16.	
5.		17.	
6.		18.	
7.		19.	
8.		20.	
9.		21.	
10.		22.	
11.		23.	
12.		24.	

Roots and Beyond

Directions: Look at the words in columns *Example 1* and *Example 2*. Write the root word in the first column. Then think of another word with the same root word but a different prefix or suffix. Write it in the column *Example 3*. The first row of the chart is done for you.

Root Word	Example 1	Example 2	Example 3
sleep	sleepily	sleepy	sleeper
	helpless	helpful	
	wonderer	wondering	
	redo	undo	
	tiresome	retire	
	misspell	speller	
	misread	readable	
	befriend	friendship	
	interlocking	locker	
	correctly	incorrect	
	midfield	fielder	
	director	indirect	
	overplay	player	
	retract	traction	
	dreamily	dreaming	

Directions: Now think of three more root words. Add a different suffix and prefix to make three new words from each root word.

Root Word	Word 1	Word 2	Word 3

Latin Roots Match Game

Play the following game to introduce students to Latin roots and enable them to figure out meanings of words that contain those roots.

Write the words *ambiguous* and *ambidextrous* on the board. Ask students to define the words. Then underline the Latin root (i.e., *ambi*) in each word. Ask students to guess the meaning of the root. Then challenge them to think of other words that contain the root (e.g., *ambivalent*). Repeat these steps with other words derived from Latin roots, such as *fracture* and *fraction*.

Refer to the **Latin Roots Chart reproducible (page 67)**. For each root in the *Latin Root* column, prepare two corresponding index cards. Write the definition of the Latin root on one card. Write examples of words derived from that root on the other index card and underline the root. Shuffle the cards.

Give each student a card. Tell students that they need to find their partner by matching the definition with the correct Latin root on the corresponding card. For example, the student with the card showing *water* will pair up with the student holding the card showing *aqua*rium and *aqua*marine.

After students have found their partners, call on each pair to share their words with the class. Tell students to identify the Latin root and what the root means. Have students in each pair share their respective cards so that everyone has a chance to speak.

Copy a class set of the Latin Roots Chart reproducible. Hand out the chart and explain to students that it shows the Latin root, the definition of the root, and examples of words containing the root. Review the first example (i.e., *ambi*) with them to be sure everyone understands how to use the chart. Ask students to store the chart where they can refer to it often and encourage them to use it to figure out the meanings of unfamiliar words.

Encourage students to continue practicing with Latin roots by completing the **Latin Roots Match-Up reproducible (page 68)**. Invite students to peer-check each other's work for accuracy.

Latin Roots Chart

Latin Root	Definition	Examples
ambi	both	ambiguous, ambidextrous
aqua	water	aquarium, aquamarine
aud	to hear	audience, audition
bene	good	benefactor, benevolent
cent	one hundred	century, percent
circum	around	circumference, circumstance
contra/counter	against	contradict, encounter
dict	to say	dictation, dictator
duc/duct	to lead	conduct, induce
fac	to do; to make	factory, manufacture
form	shape	conform, reform
fort	strength	fortitude, fortress
fract	to break	fracture, fraction
ject	throw	projection, rejection
jud	judge	judicial, prejudice
mal	bad	malevolent, malefactor
mater	mother	maternal, maternity
mit	to send	transmit, admit
mort	death	mortal, mortician
multi	many	multimedia, multiple
pater	father	paternal, paternity
port	to carry	portable, transportation
rupt	to break	bankrupt, disruption
scrib/script	to write	inscription, prescribe
sect/sec	to cut	bisect, section
sent	to feel; to send	consent, resent
spect	to look	inspection, spectator
struct	to build	destruction, restructure
vid/vis	to see	televise, video
voc	voice; to call	vocalize, advocate

Latin Roots Match-Up

Directions: Match each Latin root with its meaning. The first one is done for you.

1. __I__ multi   **A.** to carry
2. ____ ambi   **B.** father
3. ____ scrib/script   **C.** to look
4. ____ port   **D.** to hear
5. ____ mort   **E.** around
6. ____ ject   **F.** both
7. ____ voc   **G.** throw
8. ____ cent   **H.** shape

9. ____ bene   **I.** many
10. ____ aud   **J.** voice; to call
11. ____ mal   **K.** to send
12. ____ pater   **L.** good
13. ____ spect   **M.** death
14. ____ mit   **N.** one hundred
15. ____ form   **O.** bad
16. ____ circum   **P.** to write

Directions: Read each word in the left column. Refer to your Latin Roots Chart. Write the Latin root in the middle column and the definition of the root in the right column.

Word	Latin Root	Definition
17. dictation	_____	_____
18. conduct	_____	_____
19. prejudice	_____	_____
20. disruption	_____	_____
21. structure	_____	_____
22. contradict	_____	_____
23. video	_____	_____
24. manufacture	_____	_____
25. maternal	_____	_____
26. fortress	_____	_____

Greek Roots Match Game

Play the following game to introduce students to Greek roots and enable them to figure out meanings of words that contain those roots.

Write the words *anthropologist* and *philanthropy* on the board. Ask students to define the words. Then underline the Greek root (i.e., *anthropo*) in each word. Ask students to guess the meaning of the root. Then challenge students to think of other words that contain the root (e.g., *anthropology*). Repeat these steps with other words derived from Greek roots, such as *graphic* and *phonograph*.

Refer to the **Greek Roots Chart reproducible (page 70)**. For each root in the *Greek Root* column, prepare two corresponding index cards. Write the definition of the Greek root on one card. Write examples of words derived from that root on the other index card and underline the root. Shuffle the cards.

Give each student a card. Tell students that they need to find their partner by matching the definition with the correct Greek root on the corresponding card. For example, the student with the card showing *water* will pair up with the student holding the card showing *hydration* and *dehydrate*.

After students have found their partners, call on each pair to share their words with the class. Tell students to identify the Greek root and what the root means. Have students in each pair share their respective cards so that everyone has a chance to speak.

Copy a class set of the Greek Roots Chart reproducible. Hand out the chart and explain to students that it shows the Greek root, the definition of the root, and examples of words containing the root. Review the first example (i.e., *anthropo*) with them to be sure everyone understands how to use the chart. Ask students to store the chart where they can refer to it often and encourage them to use it to figure out the meanings of unfamiliar words.

Encourage students to continue practicing with Greek roots by completing the **Greek Roots Match-Up reproducible (page 71)**. Invite students to peer-check each other's work for accuracy.

Greek Roots Chart

Greek Root	Definition	Examples
anthropo	man; human; humanity	anthropologist, philanthropy
auto	self	autobiography, automobile
bio	life	biology, biography
chron	time	chronological, chronic
dyna	power	dynamic, dynamite
dys	bad; hard; unlucky	dysfunctional, dyslexic
gram	thing written	epigram, telegram
graph	writing	graphic, phonograph
hetero	different	heteronym, heterogeneous
homo	same	homonym, homogenous
hydr	water	hydration, dehydrate
hyper	over; above; beyond	hyperactive, hyperbole
hypo	below; beneath	hypothermia, hypothetical
logy	study of	biology, psychology
meter/metr	measure	thermometer, perimeter
micro	small	microbe, microscope
mis/miso	hate	misanthrope, misogyny
mono	one	monologue, monotonous
morph	form; shape	morphology, morphing
nym	name	antonym, synonym
phil	love	philanthropist, philosophy
phobia	fear	claustrophobia, phobic
phon	sound	phone, symphony
photo/phos	light	photograph, phosphorus
pseudo	false	pseudonym, pseudoscience
psycho	soul; spirit	psychology, psychic
scope	viewing instrument	microscope, telescope
techno	art; science; skill	technique, technological
tele	far off	television, telephone
therm	heat	thermal, thermometer

Greek Roots Match-Up

Directions: Match each Greek root with its meaning. The first one is done for you.

1. _G_ chron	**A.** form; shape		9. ____ phil	**I.** measure		
2. ____ meter	**B.** fear		10. ____ mono	**J.** over; above; beyond		
3. ____ hyper	**C.** study of		11. ____ dys	**K.** heat		
4. ____ graph	**D.** name		12. ____ nym	**L.** life		
5. ____ psycho	**E.** viewing instrument		13. ____ phobia	**M.** soul; spirit		
6. ____ therm	**F.** bad; hard; unlucky		14. ____ scope	**N.** one		
7. ____ logy	**G.** time		15. ____ bio	**O.** love		
8. ____ micro	**H.** small		16. ____ morph	**P.** writing		

Directions: Read each word in the left column. Refer to your Greek Roots Chart. Write the Greek root in the middle column and the definition of the root in the right column.

Word	Greek Root	Definition
17. hypothetical	_____	_____
18. symphony	_____	_____
19. misanthrope	_____	_____
20. dehydrate	_____	_____
21. homonym	_____	_____
22. phosphorous	_____	_____
23. dynamic	_____	_____
24. pseudonym	_____	_____
25. telegram	_____	_____
26. autobiography	_____	_____

Latin and Greek Roots Practice

This exercise continues to build on the introduction to Latin and Greek roots that will enable students to figure out meanings of words that contain those roots.

Refer to the Latin Roots Chart and Greek Roots Chart reproducibles (pages 67 and 70). Write on the board or overhead any five words or sets of words from the *Examples* columns. Ask students if they can remember the roots and meanings of the roots of those words. Then ask students if they know any other words that contain these roots and what those words mean.

Tell students to refer to their Latin Roots and Greek Roots Charts. Ask a student to select a word or set of words from the *Examples* columns. Review with the class how to read the charts (students should understand that the charts show the root, the definition of the root, and examples of words containing the root).

Make several copies of the **Reaching for Roots reproducible (page 73)** for each student. Write the following word list on the board:

biology	*thermometer*
photograph	*television*
microscope	*homonym*
autobiography	*contradict*
benefactor	*telegram*

Explain that each word in the list is made up of roots from either or both of the Latin Roots and Greek Roots Charts. Show students that every word has two roots, and one of the words has three roots. Place a transparency of the Reaching for Roots reproducible on the overhead. Demonstrate how to complete the graphic organizer. Start by writing a word in the trunk of the tree. Write the first root in the appropriate box and provide its meaning. Do the same for the second and third root if necessary. Finally, write a definition in the box at the bottom of the page. Repeat the same procedure for other words on the list.

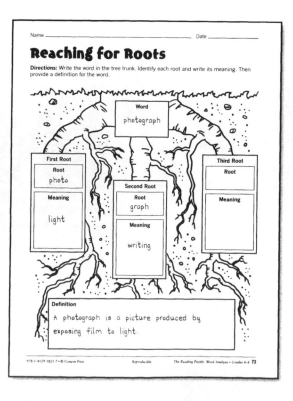

Reaching for Roots

Directions: Write the word in the tree trunk. Identify each root and write its meaning. Then provide a definition for the word.

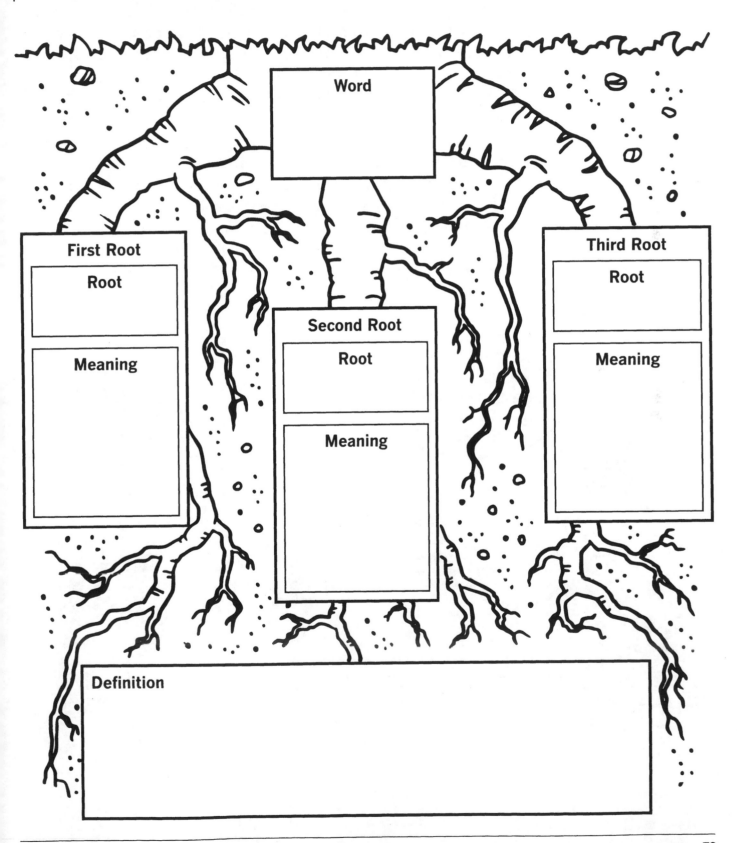

Using Roots in Sentences

Give students the opportunity to write original sentences using words containing Latin and Greek roots from their charts.

Have students take out their Greek Roots and Latin Roots Charts. Call on a student and ask for the definition of the root *fract*. Call on another student to use one of the examples for *fract* (or any other word containing that root) correctly in a sentence. Write the student's word on the board and call on another student to underline the root in the word. Continue with other roots and their definitions.

Copy a class set of the **Using Roots in Sentences reproducible (page 75)** and distribute them to students. Read the directions on the reproducible with students and go through the example provided. Remind students that the procedure is similar to what they did in class.

Provide students with more opportunities to practice with Latin and Greek roots. Give them a copy the **Mina's Dream Job** and **Identify the Roots reproducibles (pages 76–77)**. First, have students read the story "Mina's Dream Job," and then use the words from the story to complete the Identify the Roots reproducible.

Using Roots in Sentences

Directions: Write the meaning of the root. Then write a sentence using a word with that root. You may use your Latin Roots and Greek Roots Charts. Circle the root in your word.

Root	Definition	Sentence
1. ambi	both	We were confused by Felipe's (ambi)guous statements.
2. aud		
3. ject		
4. pseudo		
5. mono		
6. phon		
7. circum		
8. graph		
9. vis		
10. fort		
11. hyper		
12. port		
13. sect		
14. psycho		
15. struct		

Name _____ Date _____

Mina's Dream Job

Directions: As you read the story, use your knowledge of Latin and Greek roots to think about the meanings of the boldface words. Then complete the Identify the Roots reproducible.

As a little girl, Mina would sit on the beach with her **telescope** and look out to sea. Sometimes, like a spectator at a sporting event, she would search for her **dynamic** heroes: dolphins and whales. Sometimes she would try to **visualize** the **multitudes** beneath the water's surface. On special evenings when conditions were right, she would watch the bursts of **phosphorescence produced** from the **microorganisms** thrown about in the waves.

Now, almost a quarter of a **century** later, Mina put her interest in marine **biology** to good use. She was working at an **aquarium** in California on a **project** funded through the **benevolence** of a local **philanthropist**. Much of the work was rather **monotonous**. Often, she simply took **thermometer** readings and **constructed** basic **diagrams**. Nevertheless, her **circumstances** were good, even if she could not **dictate** all of the conditions of her job.

Mina's **telephone** rang. It was her father, a well-known **psychology** expert who also published novels under a **pseudonym**. Would she **consent** to have lunch with him today?

Mina knew that it would **disrupt** her work schedule, but she could always use some **paternal** advice. After a less than **hyperactive** morning spent labeling test tubes and placing them in **chronological** order, this lunch date was a welcome relief. It was just what she would have **prescribed** for herself had she thought of it first!

Before Mina's father could **vocalize** his thoughts any further, she suggested where and when they would meet, leaving plenty of time to return for the afternoon show. Her father did not **contradict** her.

Her father listened to her and encouraged her to focus on the positive aspects of her job. Mina returned for the afternoon aquarium show. She loved this part of her job more than anything. Each **audience** was different and exciting in its own way, and Mina **committed** herself to the **performance**. If she was ever **ambivalent** about how a show was going, all she had to do was look out over the water for a few moments at the dolphins as they displayed their natural talents. After all these years, these animals still fascinated her and gave her great joy.

Identify the Roots

Directions: Review the boldface words in the story "Mina's Dream Job." Write the root(s) from each of those words next to the matching definition below.

Boldface Word	Definition	Root(s)
1.	people who listen to or hear	
2.	study of living things	
3.	creatures that light up in the dark	
4.	false name	
5.	speak against	
6.	in order by time	
7.	instrument for viewing from afar	
8.	fatherly	
9.	written sketches	
10.	call out or speak	
11.	situation around someone	
12.	break up a pattern	
13.	lover of humanity	
14.	device for measuring heat	
15.	one hundred years	

Directions: Choose two new boldface words from story. Use each word in a sentence.

16. _____

17. _____

Affixes

Prefix and Suffix Patterns

While a prefix changes the meaning of the root word, it typically does not change the part of speech.

A suffix, however, not only changes the meaning of the root word, but it often changes the part of speech as well.

Introduction to Affixes

One method of understanding the meanings of new words is to analyze the different parts of the word and the meanings of those parts. Many new words are formed by adding a morphograph to the beginning or end of a Latin or Greek root or root word. Often, both beginning and ending syllables are added.

These morphographs, called *affixes*, have their own separate meanings. When they are added to the beginning of roots or root words, they are called *prefixes*. For example, the most common prefix is *un-*, which means *not* or *opposite of*. For example, if you add *un-* to the word *happy*, the new word becomes *unhappy*, which means *not happy*.

While a prefix changes the meaning of the root word, it typically does not change the part of speech. For example, both *happy* and *unhappy* are adjectives; both *prove* and *improve* are verbs. Note that the spelling of the prefix and the root word do not change.

When affixes are added to the end of roots or root words, they are called *suffixes*. For example, the most common suffixes are *-s* and *-es*. These are added to a root word to indicate more than one (or the plural) of the word. If you add *-s* to *home*, the meaning of the word changes to *more than one home*; if you add *-es* to *wish*, the meaning of the word changes to *more than one wish*.

A suffix not only changes the meaning of the root word, but it often changes the part of speech as well. For example, although *home* and *homes* are both nouns, if you add the suffix *-less* to *home*, the word *homeless* is an adjective. If you add the suffix *-ful* to *wish*, the word *wishful* is an adjective. When adding a suffix to a root word, the end spelling of that root word will often also change.

Understanding the meanings of affixes enables students to figure out the meanings of new words, especially when used in conjunction with knowledge of Greek and Latin roots and root words. More than 100 different prefixes and 100 different suffixes exist. This chapter contains charts that identify the 20 most common prefixes and the 20 most common suffixes. These lists account for most of the words students will encounter.

When finished with this section, challenge students to invent a game to perfect their knowledge of affixes. If you wish, have them use the games "Understanding Pronunciation Patterns" and "Mastering Pronunciation Patterns" (pages 49–55) as models for their games.

Prefixes in a Flash

In this exercise, students will create flashcards in order to practice learning prefixes and their meanings. All groups will use the same list of prefixes, so they will create the same sets of flashcards and practice the same sets of prefixes.

Copy a class set of the **Common Prefixes reproducible (page 80)**. Divide the class into groups of four. Give each group member a number (i.e., *1, 2, 3,* or *4*). Hand out the Common Prefixes reproducible, 20 index cards, and four markers per group. Tell the class that Student 1 in each group will make flashcards for the first five prefixes. Ask students to use a marker to write the prefix on one side of the index card and the definition on the other side. Have Student 2 make cards for the second five prefixes, Student 3 the third five prefixes, and Student 4 the last five prefixes.

When students have finished their cards, have each group member pair up with one partner. Tell students to drill their partners about prefixes and their meanings using the flashcards. Tell partners to continue until they can identify the five prefixes and definitions perfectly.

Then ask students to pair off with a different group member and repeat the process. After a few minutes, tell them to repeat the process with their final partner. After a few more minutes, have final partners exchange cards and repeat the process so that every student practices all 20 prefixes. Have students bind their sets of cards together with a rubber band. Collect all the cards.

Now do choral practice with the entire group, going through the Common Prefixes list until you are satisfied that students can define the terms. Call on individual students to read and define prefixes at random.

Provide students with additional practice with prefixes by having them complete the **I Get Your Meaning, Prefix Hopscotch, Max's Dream**, and **Prefixes on Your Own reproducibles (pages 81–84)**.

Common Prefixes

A **prefix** is a morphograph that is added to the front of a root or root word to create a new word with a new meaning.

The chart below displays 20 commonly used prefixes.

Prefix	Definition	Examples
anti-	against	anticlimax
de-	opposite	devalue
dis-	not; opposite of	discover
en-, em-	cause to	enact, empower
fore-	before; front of	foreshadow, forearm
in-, im-	in	income, impulse
in-, im-, il-, ir-	not	indirect, immoral, illiterate, irreverent
inter-	between; among	interrupt
mid-	middle	midfield
mis-	wrongly	misspell
non-	not	nonviolent
over-	over; too much	overeat
pre-	before	preview
re-	again	rewrite
semi-	half; partly, not fully	semifinal
sub-	under	subway
super-	above; beyond	superhuman
trans-	across	transmit
un-	not; opposite of	unusual
under-	under; too little	underestimate

Name _____ Date _____

I Get Your Meaning

Directions: Write one or more prefix from the Common Prefixes chart next to its definition.

Definition	Suffix(es)	Definition	Suffix(es)
not or opposite of		above; beyond	
		again	
		against	
		across	
		before	
wrongly			
over		between; among	
middle		in	
under		half; partly	
too little		cause to	

Directions: Write each word from the box next to its definition.

antibody	deport	displace	foretell	illiterate	import
interfaith	misplace	nonviolent	overthrow	prepaid	replace
semiliterate	subhuman	superhuman	unable	undercharge	midfield

1. place wrongly _____

2. beyond human _____

3. not violent _____

4. throw too much _____

5. not literate _____

6. place again _____

7. opposite of port _____

8. between faiths _____

9. below human _____

10. middle of the field _____

11. tell before _____

12. not able _____

13. bring in _____

14. half literate _____

15. opposite of place _____

16. charge too little _____

17. against the body _____

18. paid before _____

Prefix Hopscotch

Directions: In the hopscotch pattern, write the prefix that will form a word with the word part below it. Then write the correct prefix next to the root or root word on the left.

1. de-   en-   _____ able
2. inter-   in-   _____ state
3. im-   un-   _____ possible
4. fore-   inter-   _____ head
5. mis-   de-   _____ understand
6. il-   ir-   _____ regular
7. dis-   sub-   _____ cover
8. un-   pre-   _____ view
9. dis-   un-   _____ acceptable
10. anti-   over-   _____ rated
11. il-   un-   _____ logical
12. trans-   semi-   _____ port
13. sub-   under-   _____ marine
14. semi-   over-   _____ final

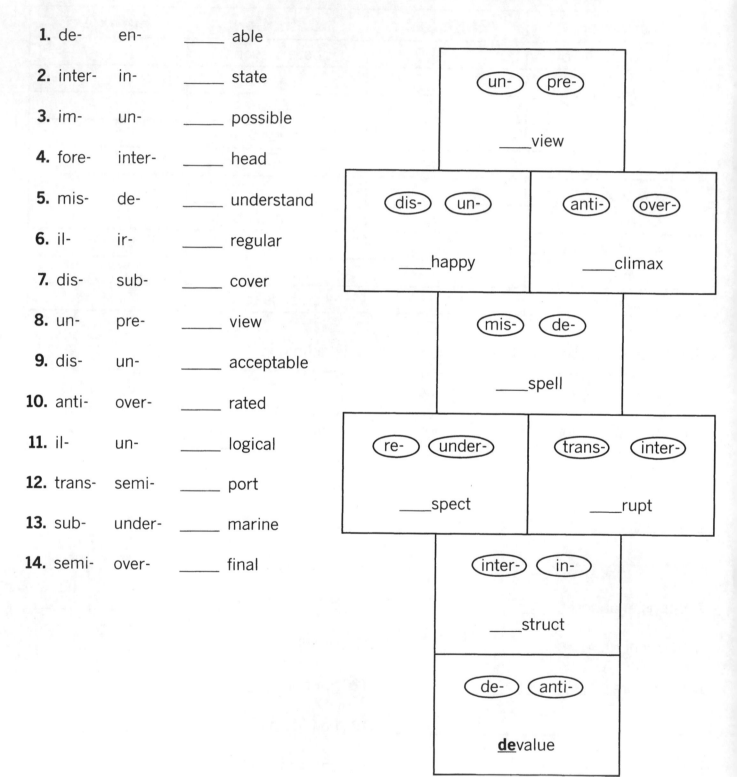

un-   pre-

____view

dis-   un-   anti-   over-

____happy   ____climax

mis-   de-

____spell

re-   under-   trans-   inter-

____spect   ____rupt

inter-   in-

____struct

de-   anti-

devalue

Name _____.　　　　　　Date _____

Max's Dream

Directions: Read each sentence. Write the meaning of the underlined word on the line. Use your Common Prefixes chart to help you.

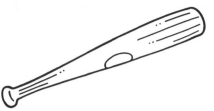

1. Max's dream was to become a baseball <u>superstar</u>.

   Superstar means <u>beyond a star</u>

2. In order to improve his skills, he <u>reviewed</u> his performance after every game.

   Reviewed means _____

3. If he thought his play was <u>substandard</u>, Max would practice harder.

   Substandard means _____

4. If he <u>misunderstood</u> a signal from the coach, he would study them again.

   Misunderstood means _____

5. After all, he did not want the coach to think he was <u>irresponsible</u>.

   Irresponsible means _____

6. He also did not want his teammates to think that he was <u>unintelligent</u>.

   Unintelligent means _____

7. Before the next <u>interleague</u> game, he needed to buy some new equipment.

   Interleague means _____

8. Max wanted to show his parents that he would not <u>overspend</u> his budget.

   Overspend means _____

9. He did not want them to think that he was too <u>immature</u> to make money decisions.

   Immature means _____

10. With much <u>forethought</u>, Max bought everything he needed to continue pursuing his dream.

    Forethought means _____

Prefixes on Your Own

Directions: Write a word that begins with each prefix below. Then use your knowledge of prefixes to write the meaning of the word.

Prefix	Example	Your Word	Your Word's Meaning
anti-	antibody		
de-	deprogram		
dis-	displace		
en-, em-	embody		
fore-	foretell		
in-, im-	improve		
in-, im-, il-, ir-	illegal		
inter-	interfaith		
mid-	midlife		
mis-	misfire		
non-	nonentity		
over-	overboard		
pre-	prepaid		
re-	recall		
semi-	semicolon		
sub-	subhuman		
super-	superman		
trans-	transport		
un-	unable		
under-	undergo		

Suffixes in a Flash

In this exercise, students will create flashcards in order to practice learning suffixes and their meanings. Groups will use the same list of suffixes, so they will create the same sets of flashcards and practice the same sets of suffixes.

Copy a class set of the **Common Suffixes reproducible (page 86)**. Divide the class into groups of four. Give each group member a number (i.e., *1, 2, 3,* or *4*). Hand out the Common Suffixes reproducible, 20 index cards, and four markers per group. Tell the class that Student 1 in each group will make flashcards for the first five suffixes. Ask students to use a marker to write the suffix on one side of the index card and the definition on the other side. Have Student 2 make cards for the second five suffixes, Student 3 the third five suffixes, and Student 4 the last five suffixes.

When students have finished their cards, have each group member pair up with one partner. Tell students to drill their partners about suffixes and their meanings using the flashcards. Tell partners to continue until they can identify the five suffixes and definitions perfectly.

Then ask students to pair off with a different group member and repeat the process. After a few minutes, tell them to repeat the process with their final partner. After a few more minutes, have final partners exchange cards and repeat the process so that every student practices all 20 suffixes. Have students bind their sets of cards together with a rubber band. Collect all the cards.

Now do choral practice with the entire group, going through the Common Suffixes list until you are satisfied that students can define the terms. Call on individual students to read and define suffixes at random.

Provide students with additional practice with suffixes by having them complete the **I Still Get Your Meaning, The Disappearing Letters, Max's Dream Continues,** and **Suffixes on Your Own reproducibles (pages 87–90)**.

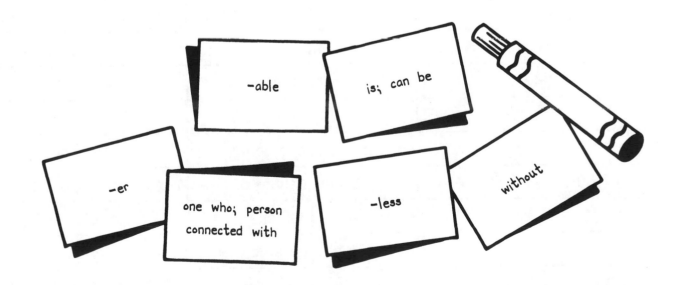

Common Suffixes

A **suffix** is a morphograph that is added to the end of a root or root word to create a new word with a new meaning.

The chart below displays 20 commonly used suffixes.

Suffix	Definition	Examples
-able, -ible	is; can be	affordable, sensible
-al, -ial	having characteristics of	universal, facial
-ed	past tense verbs; adjectives	the dog walked, the walked dog
-en	made of	golden
-er, -or	one who; person connected with	teacher, professor
-er	more	taller
-est	the most	tallest
-ful	full of	helpful
-ic	having characteristics of	poetic
-ing	verb forms; present participles	sleeping
-ion, -tion, -ation, -ition	act; process	submission, motion, relation, edition
-ity, -ty	state of	activity, society
-ive, -ative, -itive	adjective form of noun	active, comparative, sensitive
-less	without	hopeless
-ly	how something is	lovely
-ment	state of being; act of	contentment
-ness	state of; condition of	openness
-ous, -eous, -ious	having qualities of	riotous, courageous, gracious
-s, -es	more than one	trains, trenches
-y	characterized by	gloomy

Reproducible   978-1-4129-5825-7 • © Corwin Press

Name _____ Date _____

I Still Get Your Meaning

Directions: Write one or more suffix from the Common Suffixes chart next to its definition.

Definition	Suffix(es)	Definition	Suffix(es)
having characteristics of		is; can be	
		more than one	
characterized by		adjective form of noun	
act; process		one who	
state of being; act of		how something is	
the most		more	
full of		having qualities of	
made of		without	
state of		past tense	
		present participle	

Directions: Write each word from the box next to its definition.

blended	discoverer	doable	effective	development	expression
flowers	gladly	greatest	healthy	oaken	plentiful
sadness	sanity	smarter	spacious	worthless	wrecking

1. without worth _____

2. state of being sane _____

3. act of expressing _____

4. most great _____

5. characterized by health _____

6. state of being sad _____

7. past tense of *blend* _____

8. full of plenty _____

9. one who discovers _____

10. made of oak _____

11. how glad _____

12. act of developing _____

13. more than one flower _____

14. can be done _____

15. adjective form of *effect* _____

16. more smart _____

17. present participle of *wreck* _____

18. having qualities of space _____

The Disappearing Letters

Directions: When an ending, or suffix, is added to a root word that ends in *e* or *y*, those letters may change or drop from the newly formed word. In the story below, each boldface word contains a root word that ends in *e* or *y*. Read the story and then write each boldface word next to its root word. Circle the suffix.

Graham R. Ecksbert, private **investigator**, was **busily** working on his latest case. The well-known soup maker, Chick N. Udell, had been **receiving** complaints from the Alphabet Soup **Division**. They were **continually** running out of the letter *p*. As a result, they could not guarantee that all of the cans they were **preparing** contained every letter of the alphabet. If this continued on a **daily** basis, there were bound to be **inquiries** from their customers. It did not take much **imagination** to realize how this would be bad for business.

Not **surprisingly**, Graham was again able to solve the case with **comparative** ease. As **unbelievable** as it may seem, a worker named Pee Wee Pease from the Pea Soup Division had misunderstood his orders for **making** pea soup. He had been told to begin **saving** all of the peas he could. Because he thought the order meant the letter *p*, he had gone to the Alphabet Soup Division and was **taking** all of the *p*'s they used in their alphabet soup. Graham thought this was one of the **silliest** cases he had ever solved, but Chick N. Udell received the news with great **happiness**. Soon, he was again **noisily advertising** that you could **easily** find every letter in every can of his alphabet soup.

1. advertise _____

2. inquire _____

3. believe _____

4. investigate _____

5. busy _____

6. make _____

7. compare _____

8. noise _____

9. continue _____

10. prepare _____

11. day _____

12. receive _____

13. divide _____

14. save _____

15. ease _____

16. silly _____

17. happy _____

18. surprise _____

19. imagine _____

20. take _____

Name _____ Date _____

Max's Dream Continues

Directions: Read each sentence. Write the meaning of the underlined word on the line. Use your Common Suffixes chart to help you.

1. As Max grew older, he devoted <u>endless</u> hours to practicing his skills.

   Endless means <u>without end</u>

2. It wasn't long before <u>professional</u> baseball teams began to show an interest in him.

   Professional means _____

3. They admired his <u>ability</u> to read plays and keep a cool head under pressure.

   Ability means _____

4. One scout described Max as "the most <u>effective</u> team player I have ever seen."

   Effective means _____

5. The <u>management</u> of that team was soon in contact with him.

   Management means _____

6. They told Max how much they wanted him to join their <u>organization</u>.

   Organization means _____

7. Max imagined what it would be like to be a <u>famous</u> baseball player.

   Famous means _____

8. He also, however, wanted to be <u>careful</u> about making a good decision.

   Careful means _____

9. The coach was <u>comfortable</u> with the team's offer.

   Comfortable means _____

10. As Max signed his contract the following day, he could scarcely contain his <u>happiness</u>.

    Happiness means _____

Suffixes on Your Own

Write a word that ends with each suffix below. Then use your knowledge of suffixes to write the meaning of the word.

Suffix	Example	Your Word	Your Word's Meaning
-able, -ible	transferable		
-al, -ial	social		
-ed	smiled		
-en	waxen		
-er, -or	baker		
-er	bolder		
-est	cleanest		
-ful	graceful		
-ic	aerobic		
-ing	stamping		
-ion, -tion	demonstration		
-ation, -ition	admission		
-ity, -ty	responsibility		
-ive, -ative	imaginative		
-itive	repetitive		
-less	thoughtless		
-ly	openly		
-ment	experiment		
-ness	fullness		
-ous, -eous	perilous		
-ious	continuous		
-s, -es	foxes		
-y	tasty		

Papa V. Nic

Adding suffixes can change a word's part of speech, but sometimes it is hard for students to remember the parts of speech themselves. After students have learned the meanings of the suffixes in the Common Suffixes chart, practice putting the suffixes on root words and discuss the meanings of the new words and their parts of speech. Use the acronym and activity described below to remind students about the eight parts of speech.

Refer to the illustration below to create a poster of Papa V. Nic. Make sure your drawing has an upside-down "V" neck to help students remember the acronym for the parts of speech. Because he is a "papa," draw a moustache and an old-style cap. Write the name *Papa V. Nic* under your drawing.

Then write *Papa V. Nic* vertically down the left side of the board. Tell students that *Papa V. Nic* will help them to remember the eight parts of speech. Ask students to guess the parts of speech, while you write them next to the corresponding letters. As you write their responses, start with *pronoun* and *adjective* at the top, and keep *adverb* and *verb* together. Tell students that *prepositions* tell the position of something, and underline *position* in *preposition*.

Pronoun: word that takes the place of a noun

Adjective: word that describes a noun

Pre<u>position</u>: word that gives position

Adverb: word that describes a verb

Verb: word of action or state of being

Noun: person, place, thing, or idea

Interjection: word that expresses great emotion, such as *Help! Stop!*

Conjunction: word that joins together parts of sentences

Have students write what each part of speech does. Then direct them to copy the picture of Papa V. Nic and record his name under the picture. Have students write the acronym with the eight parts of speech. Tell them to keep Papa V. Nic where they can refer to it often.

Reward students who can remember the eight parts of speech at the end of class, the next day, and at the end of the week. Encourage students to identify and describe the parts of speech in Papa V. Nic order.

Give students a copy of the **Changing Hats reproducible (page 92)**. Invite them to practice what they learned about parts of speech by completing the reproducible.

Changing Hats

Directions: Read each sentence. Then write the part of speech of the second boldface word.

1. The young couple was in **love**, and Jim thought his wife was a **lovely** person.

   love—noun   lovely—adjective

2. Tanya could not **sleep** and had already endured many **sleepless** nights.

   sleep—verb   sleepless—_____

3. Roberto's team was **happy** when they finished in first place, but their **happiness** was not complete until they won the league championship.

   happy—adjective   happiness—_____

4. Cassie can **sing** beautifully and dreams of becoming a professional **singer**.

   sing—verb   singer—_____

5. Peri's Pets did not make a **profit** its first year but soon after became very **profitable**.

   profit—noun   profitable—_____

6. If you do not **enjoy** movies, you may find **enjoyment** in reading the book instead.

   enjoy—verb   enjoyment—_____

7. As a nurse, Ivan **helped** many patients; he was known as extremely **helpful**.

   helped—verb   helpful—_____

8. The **builders** have not decided when they will **build** the new bridge.

   builders—noun   build—_____

9. The congressmen at the **table** finally **tabled** action on the bill.

   table—noun   tabled—_____

10. Even if you **teach** yourself a skill, a **teacher** can still help you improve it.

    teach—verb   teacher—_____

Answer Key

I KNOW MY CONSONANT PAIRS (PAGE 8)
1. p
2. d
3. f
4. z
5. k
6. noisy
7. noisy
8. noisy
9. quiet
10. noisy
11. noisy
12. quiet
13. quiet
14. quiet
15. quiet
16. C
17. B
18. A
19. E
20. D

WORD SORT REVIEW (PAGE 19)
ch
/ch/—teacher, each, approached, challenge, checked, charm, pinch, chocolate, cherries, arched, speech, chalk, exchange, cheeks
/sh/—Charlotte, chef, caches
/k/—scholarship, character, chemistry, bellyache, school's, school, chlorine

ea
/ĕ/—head, Heather, measure, heavy, bread, breakfast, weather, heads
/ē/—teacher, each, easy, cream, eat, clear, sea, Beneath, leafy, daydreaming, daydream, please, hear

ed
/t/—approached, checked, arched, looked, clipped, stopped, piped
/d/—assigned, discovered, brewed, showed, lined, combined, roused, turned, burned, mouthed
/əd/—added, reminded, greeted, wanted, uninterested, cemented, started, created

s
/s/—assigned, desks, across, class, smile, scholarship, simple, discovered, chemistry, salt, breakfast, experiments, glass, sea, sometimes, grassy, school's, bikes, uninterested, speech, school, Miss, started, answer, stopped, cheeks, let's, thoughts, Thanks, it's, that's
/z/—girls, friends, easy, as, was, numbers, cherries, nose, mixtures, things, recipes, room's, sometimes, school's, fields, trees, caches, owners, was, exclamations, roused, always, please, heads, rosy, friend's, always, because, numbers

PROUD CROWS AND OWLS (PAGE 31)
/ou/—cloud, pouch, round, mouth, crown, growl, shout, howl, down, proud, crowd, mound, gown, round, town, loud, frown, count, wound, doubt

/ō/—thrown, know, grow, bowl, owner, mow, flow, arrow, borrow, yellow, low, shown, follow, glow, stow, blow, slow, show, snow, known

REVIEWING SOFT C AND HARD C (PAGE 40)
1. collect—o, t; hard
2. car—a; hard
3. climate—l; hard
4. dance—e; soft
5. construct—o, t; hard
6. curious—u; hard
7. coast—o; hard
8. city—i; soft
9. evidence—e; soft
10. microscope—r, o; hard
11. cereal—e; soft
12. citrus—i; soft
13. moccasins—c, a; hard
14. cylinder—y; soft
15. ceramic—e; soft
16. scratched—r; hard (*ch* is a digraph)
17. cinch—i; soft (*ch* is a digraph)
18. ounce—e; soft

REVIEWING SOFT G AND HARD G (PAGE 47)
1. grand—r; hard
2. great—r; hard
3. ago—o; hard
4. gate—a; hard
5. goblet—o; hard
6. giant—i; soft
7. gypsy—y; soft
8. germ—e; soft
9. oxygen—e; soft
10. giraffe—i; soft
11. geyser—e; hard
12. gyoza—y; hard
13. girl—i; hard
14. giggle—i, g, l; hard
15. gearshift—e; hard
16. goal—o; hard
17. gentle—e; soft
18. geese—e; hard

UNDERSTANDING PRONUNCIATION PATTERNS (PAGE 51)
Nonsense Words with *ai* and *oa*
100 /rābōtō/
200 /gōnāsā/
300 /mābādōfā/
400 /skānātōdō/
500 /pōfādōlārāgō/

Words with *oo*
100 ŏŏ, ŏŏ, ŏŏ, ŏŏ
200 hŏŏk, ŏŏze, cŏŏkie, tŏŏth
300 shŏŏk, brŏŏk, lŏŏse, zŏŏm, hŏŏd
400 shŏŏ, snŏŏp, shŏŏk, nŏŏk, bŏŏth, wŏŏl
500 rŏŏkie, gŏŏf, bŏŏt, cŏŏk, hŏŏt, sŏŏt

Words with *ow*
100 /doun/, /thrōn/, /kloun/
200 /lō-ər/, /shou- ər/, /kou-ərd/, /hou/
300 /blōn/, /broun/, /thrōn/, /brou/
400 /doudy/, /stō/, /tō/, /wou/, /glō/
500 /vou/, /dou-ər/, /ō/, /kou-lĭk/, /bōl/

Definitions of *oa* Words
100 road
200 toast
300 toad
400 soak
500 float

Consonant Pairs
100 b
200 k, t
300 s, f, p
400 v, z, g, d
500 t, b, k, s, f

MASTERING PRONUNCIATION PATTERNS (PAGES 54–55)
Make sure students pronounce the following words correctly.

Heteronyms
200 drawer, drawings, drawer
400 moped, close, closed, moped
600 intermediate, intermediate, row, row
800 objected, dove, dove, object
1,000 resented, resent, content, content

Words with *ch*
200 coach, speechless, enchanting, school, chorus
400 scholars, Chevy, ranch, beach, search, peaches
600 chauvinistic, bachelor, fuchsia, brochure, chiropractor's, chocolate, enchiladas
800 chauffeur, character, munch, chocolate, cheese, lunch, chandelier, which, bellyache
1,000 research, chemistry, speech, scholarship, Chlorine, Cheyenne

Words with *ed*
200 looked, surprised, squatted, smelled, discovered
400 clapped, jumped, cheered, graduated, walked
600 worked, picked, decided, finished, wanted
800 crossed, blinked, stared, nodded, applauded
1,000 hoped, listened, interested, showed, curved, missed

Words with *ea*
200 dream, beneath, sea, heavy, treasure, concealed
400 breakfast, beans, bread, ready, eagles, spread, feathers
600 endeavor, wealthy, dealt, cheap, leather
800 beat, sweaty, breath, seat, clear, head
1,000 easy, beach, near, stream, lead, nearby, peak, weasel

Words with *c* Followed by *e*, *i*, or *y*
200 notice, curved, surface, bicycle's, clown, center
400 magnificent, palace, recently, discovered, celebrated, architectural
600 evidence, surfaced, calling, cell, can, cause, accident, costly, collision
800 century, Cyclops, comfortably, cylinder, tropical, climate, cirrus, clouds, centipede, circling, cylinder's, circumference
1,000 percentage, customers, escalator, cinema, comedy, conscious, concerned, citizens, moccasins, danced, spruce, circulation

ONLY THE SPELLING IS THE SAME (PAGE 61)
1. 6; number
2. 18; dove
3. 14; produce
4. 13; wind
5. 5; sow
6. 9; desert
7. 17; close
8. 1; wind
9. 11; rebel
10. 2; produce
11. 12; desert
12. 19; sow
13. 8; affect
14. 15; minute
15. 10; dove
16. 3; number
17. 20; affect
18. 7; minute
19. 4; close
20. 16; rebel

THE NATURE OF NATURE (PAGE 62)
Note: There are 40 different heteronyms. *Tower* is used three times, and *row* is used twice. 43 words are boldface.

978-1-4129-5825-7

Answer Key

PAGE 62 (CONT.)

entrance, produce, invalid, permit, desert, Row, row, <u>towers</u>, bow, tear, <u>refused</u>, lead, moped, close, close, excuse, object, <u>objected</u>, wound, <u>towers</u>, minute, minute, console, conflict, Content, moderate, content, <u>presented</u>, permit, resort, converse, invalid, wind, <u>deliberately</u>, dove, <u>towers</u>, agape, excuse, <u>attributes</u>, <u>entranced</u>, number, perfect, resort

MISTER ROJO (PAGE 64)

1. shining; shine
2. brightly; bright
3. glistened; glisten
4. skipped; skip
5. parents; parent
6. hurried; hurry
7. excitement; excite
8. filled; fill
9. finally; final
10. arrived; arrive
11. entered; enter
12. barking; bark
13. dogs; dog
14. noticed; notice
15. eyes; eye
16. immediately; immediate
17. carefully; careful (care)
18. gently; gentle
19. unhappy; happy
20. wishing; wish
21. wagging; wag
22. grinning; grin
23. broadly; broad
24. going; go

ROOTS AND BEYOND (PAGE 65)

Answers will vary.

help—helper; helped
wonder—wonderful; wondered
do—doable; doing
tire—tired; tireless
spell—spelling; spelled
read—reader; reading
friend—friendly; friendless
lock—unlock; locked
correct—correction; corrected
field—infield; fielding
direct—direction; misdirect
play—replay; display
tract—tractor; subtract
dream—dreamer; dreamy

LATIN ROOTS MATCH-UP (PAGE 68)

1. I
2. F
3. P
4. A
5. M
6. G
7. J
8. N
9. L
10. D
11. O
12. B
13. C
14. K
15. H
16. E
17. dictation—dict; to say
18. conduct—duct; to lead
19. prejudice—jud; judge
20. disruption—rupt; to break
21. structure—struct; to build
22. contradict—contra/dict; against/to say
23. video—vid; to see
24. manufacture—fac; to do; to make
25. maternal—mater; mother
26. fortress—fort; strength

GREEK ROOTS MATCH-UP (PAGE 71)

1. G
2. I
3. J
4. P
5. M
6. K
7. C
8. H
9. O
10. N
11. F
12. D
13. B
14. E
15. L
16. A
17. hypothetical—hypo; below/beneath
18. symphony—phon; sound
19. misanthrope—mis/anthropo; hate/man
20. dehydrate—hydr; water
21. homonym—homo/nym; same/name
22. phosphorus—phos; light
23. dynamic—dyna; power
24. pseudonym—pseudo/nym; false/name
25. telegram—tele/gram; far off/thing written
26. autobiography—auto/bio/graph; self/life/writing

REACHING FOR ROOTS (PAGE 73)

1. biology
   Roots and Meanings: bio—life; logy—study of
   Definition: study of life
2. photograph
   Roots and Meanings: photo—light; graph—writing
   Definition: writing with light
3. microscope
   Roots and Meanings: micro—small; scope—viewing instrument
   Definition: instrument used for viewing small things
4. autobiography
   Roots and Meanings: auto—self; bio—life; graph—writing
   Definition: writing about oneself
5. benefactor
   Roots and Meanings: bene—good; fact—to do; or—one who
   Definition: one who does good acts
6. thermometer
   Roots and Meanings: therm—heat; meter—measure
   Definition: measure heat
7. aqueduct
   Roots and Meanings: aqua—water; duct—to lead
   Definition: lead water
8. homonym
   Roots and Meanings: homo—same; nym—name
   Definition: same name (two meanings)
9. contradict
   Roots and Meanings: contra—against; dict—to say
   Definition: to say against
10. telegraph
    Roots and Meanings: tele—far; graph—thing written
    Definition: thing written from afar

USING ROOTS IN SENTENCES (PAGE 75)

Sentences will vary.

1. ambi—both; We were confused by Felipe's (**ambi**)guous statements.
2. aud—to hear; The (**audi**)ence gave a standing ovation.
3. ject—throw; The irate coach was e(**ject**)ed from the game.
4. pseudo—false; The fugitive used a (**pseudo**)nym to remain undetected.
5. mono—one; (**Mono**)tonous sounds can often put one to sleep.
6. phon—sound; We have a (**phon**)ograph that needs repair.
7. circum—around; Magellan set out to travel the earth's (**circum**)ference.
8. graph—writing; (**Graph**)ic organizers help us organize our thoughts before we write.
9. vis—to see; My (**vis**)ion was blurry after I was hit on the head.
10. fort—strength; The weaker foe was unable to penetrate the solid (**fort**)ress.
11. hyper—over; above; beyond; She began to (**hyper**)ventilate during the race.
12. port—to carry; What means of trans(**port**)ation did you take to get here?
13. sect—to cut; Our geometry teacher asked us to draw a bi(**sect**)ing line inside the triangle.
14. psycho—spirit; soul; (**Psycho**)logy is an interesting field of study.
15. struct—to build; The (**struct**)ure stood sixty feet tall.

IDENTIFY THE ROOTS (PAGE 77)

1. audience
   people who listen to or hear
   aud
2. biology
   study of living things
   bio, logy
3. phosphorescence
   light up in the dark
   phos
4. pseudonym
   false name
   pseudo, nym
5. contradict
   speak against
   contra, dict
6. chronological
   in order by time
   chron
7. telescope
   instrument for viewing from afar
   tele, scope
8. paternal
   fatherly
   pater
9. diagram
   written sketches
   gram
10. vocalize
    call out or speak
    voc
11. circumstances
    situation around someone
    circum
12. disrupt
    break up a pattern
    rupt

Answer Key

13. philanthropist
    lover of humanity
    phil, anthropo
14. thermometer
    device for measuring heat
    therm, meter
15. century
    one hundred years
    cent

I GET YOUR MEANING (PAGE 81)

Definition	Prefix(es)
not or opposite of	de
	dis
	in, im, il, ir
	non
	un
wrongly	mis
over	over
middle	mid
under	sub
too little	under

Definition	Prefix(es)
above; beyond	super
again	re
against	anti
across	trans
before	fore
	pre
between; among	inter
in	in, im
half; partly	semi
cause to	en, em

1. place wrongly—misplace
2. beyond human—superhuman
3. not violent—nonviolent
4. throw too much—overthrow
5. not literate—illiterate
6. place again—replace
7. opposite of *port*—deport
8. between faiths—interfaith
9. below human—subhuman
10. middle of the field—midfield
11. tell before—foretell
12. not able—unable
13. port in—import
14. half literate—semiliterate
15. opposite of *place*—displace
16. charge too little—undercharge
17. against the body—antibody
18. paid before—prepaid

HOPSCOTCH PREFIXES (PAGE 82)
**Hopscotch Pattern
(from top to bottom)**
preview
unhappy
anticlimax
misspell
respect
interrupt
instruct
devalue
1. enable
2. interstate
3. impossible

4. forehead
5. misunderstand
6. irregular
7. discover
8. preview
9. unacceptable
10. overrated
11. illogical
12. transport
13. submarine
14. semifinal

MAX'S DREAM (PAGE 83)
1. Superstar—beyond a star
2. Reviewed—view or look at again
3. Substandard—under or less than standard
4. Misunderstood—wrongly understood
5. Irresponsible—not responsible
6. Unintelligent—not intelligent
7. Interleague—between leagues
8. Overspend—spend too much
9. Immature—not mature
10. Forethought—think before

PREFIXES ON YOUR OWN (PAGE 84)
Answers will vary. Accept all reasonable responses.

I STILL GET YOUR MEANING (PAGE 87)

Definition	Suffix(es)
having characteristics of	al, ial
	ic
characterized by	y
act; process	ion, tion, ation, ition
state of being; act of	ment
the most	est
full of	ful
made of	en
state of	ity, ty
	ness

Definition	Suffix(es)
is; can be	able, ible
more than one	s, es
adjective form of noun	ive, ative, itive
one who	er, or
how something is	ly
more	er
having qualities of	ous, eous, ious
without	less
past tense	ed
present participle	ing

1. without worth—worthless
2. state of being sane—sanity
3. act of expressing—expression
4. most great—greatest
5. characterized by health—healthy
6. state of being sad—sadness
7. past tense of *blend*—blended
8. full of plenty—plentiful
9. one who discovers—discoverer
10. made of oak—oaken
11. how glad—gladly
12. act of developing—development
13. more than one flower—flowers
14. can be done—doable
15. adjective form of *effect*—effective
16. more smart—smarter
17. present participle of wreck—wrecking
18. having qualities of space—spacious

THE DISAPPEARING LETTERS (PAGE 88)
1. advertis**ing**
2. inquir**ies**
3. unbeliev**able**
4. investigat**or**
5. busi**ly**
6. mak**ing**
7. compar**ative**
8. noisi**ly**
9. continual**ly**
10. prepar**ing**
11. dai**ly**
12. receiv**ing**
13. divis**ion**
14. sav**ing**
15. easi**ly**
16. silli**est**
17. happi**ness**
18. surpris**ingly**
19. imagina**tion**
20. tak**ing**

MAX'S DREAM CONTINUES (PAGE 89)
1. Endless—without end
2. Professional—having characteristics of a profession
3. Ability—state of being able
4. Effective—adjective form of *effect*
5. Management—that which is managing
6. Organization—process of organizing
7. Famous—having qualities of fame
8. Careful—full of care
9. Comfortable—is of comfort
10. Happiness—state of being happy

SUFFIXES ON YOUR OWN (PAGE 90)
Answers will vary. Accept all reasonable responses.

CHANGING HATS (PAGE 92)
1. lovely—adjective
2. sleepless—adjective
3. happiness—noun
4. singer—noun
5. profitable—adjective
6. enjoyment—noun
7. helpful—adjective
8. build—verb
9. tabled—verb
10. teacher—noun

References

The American heritage college dictionary (4th ed.). (2004). Boston, MA: Houghton Mifflin.

Bear, D., Invernizzi, M., Templeton, S., & Johnston, F. (2000). *Words their way*. Upper Saddle River, NJ: Prentice Hall.

Blevins, W. (1998). *Phonics from A to Z: A practical guide*. New York, NY: Scholastic.

Dixon, R., & Engelmann, S. (2001). *Spelling through morphographs*. Columbus, OH: SRA/McGraw-Hill.

Enchanted Learning.com. (n.d.). *African elephant*. Retrieved May 27, 2007, from http://www.enchantedlearning.com/subjects/mammals/elephant/Africancoloring.shtml.

Gander Academy. (n.d.). *Antarctica resource pages*. Retrieved June 2, 2007, from http://www.stemnet.nf.ca/CITE/antgeneral.htm.

Georgia Perimeter College, Online Writing Lab, Lawrenceville. (2007). *Common prefixes, roots, and suffixes*. Retrieved July 11, 2007, from http://www.gpc.edu/~lawowl/handouts/common-prefixes.pdf.

Greene, J. F. (2005). *Language!* Longmont, CO: Sopris West.

Gulf of Maine Research Institute. (n.d.). *Antarctica*. Retrieved June 2, 2007, from http://octopus.gma.org/surfing/antarctica/antarctica.html.

Kids' Planet. (n.d.). *African elephant*. Retrieved May 27, 2007, from http://www.kidsplanet.org/factsheets/elephant.html.

Learning Resources Center. (n.d.). *Greek and Latin roots for GRE preparation*. Retrieved July 11, 2007, from http://www.msu.edu/~defores1/gre/roots/gre_rts_afx1.htm.

Lonely Planet. (n.d.). *Nepal travel information*. Retrieved June 4, 2007, from http://www.lonelyplanet.com/worldguide/destinations/asia/nepal.

McEwan, E. K. (2002). *Teach them all to read: Catching the kids who fall through the cracks*. Thousand Oaks, CA: Corwin Press.

McEwan, E. K. (2007). *40 ways to support struggling readers in content classrooms*. Thousand Oaks, CA: Corwin Press.

More Words. (n.d.). *Words with ai*. Retrieved May 28, 2007, from http://www.morewords.com/word/ai/.

More Words. (n.d.). *Words with ch*. Retrieved May 28, 2007, from http://www.morewords.com/word/ch/.

More Words. (n.d.). *Words with ea*. Retrieved May 28, 2007, from http://www.morewords.com/word/ea/.

More Words. (n.d.). *Words with oa*. Retrieved May 28, 2007, from http://www.morewords.com/word/oa/.

National parks of the West (3rd ed.). (1996). New York, NY: Fodor's Travel Publications, Inc.

NOVA Online. (2000, November). *Antarctic almanac: Warnings from the ice*. Retrieved June 2, 2007, from http://www.pbs.org/wgbh/nova/warnings/almanac/html.

Rink Works. (n.d.). *Fun with words: Heteronyms*. Retrieved April 29, 2007, from http://www.rinkworks.com/words/heteronyms.shtml.

Scholastic. (2000). *Most common prefixes*. Retrieved March 31, 2007, from http://teacher.scholastic.com/reading/bestpractices/vocabulary/pdf/prefixes_suffixes.pdf.

Smithsonian National Zoo. (n.d.). *African elephants*. Retrieved May 27, 2007, from http://nationalzoo.si.edu/Animals/AfricanSavanna/fact-afelephant.cfm.

Vahsholtz, J. (2007, September 9). *The heteronym page*. Retrieved April 29, 2007, from http://jonv.flystrip.com/heteronym/heteronym.htm.